LANZAROTE

"Fire Island" of the Canaries

Brian Dicks

Dryad Press Limited   London

The Islands series

What have these people in common: Enid Blyton, Daniel Defoe, Robert Louis Stevenson and Roy Plomley? They have all written about islands, islands as places of adventure or fantasy. Think for a moment of the many stories or events that are associated with islands. What do you know about "Fortress Falklands", or Alcatraz, or the adventures of Robinson Crusoe? Islands have long held a special appeal and this series sets out to explore the fascination of islands.

Every island is unique, with a different location, a distinctive history and a particular personality. And yet about them all there are similarities, too. Island cultures are distinct because they are isolated, set apart from mainstream societies. They can be remote, places of refuge or sanctuary, where you can "get away from it all"! Monks and rich recluses have chosen island homes because they wanted seclusion. Other island inhabitants have had no choice in the matter because the isolation of islands also makes them ideal places for imprisonment or exile; Alcatraz and Elba certainly have that one thing in common.

In many cases, too, the remoteness of islands has meant that life for people, animals and plants has remained undisturbed by the progress and change of the mainlands. Forms and ways of life survive which elsewhere have become extinct, as is the case on the remote and beautiful islands of the Galapagos.

Another common feature of island life is that it can present similar problems of survival. Is there enough land to grow food and to keep animals? Is there an ample supply of water?

Why do islands become deserted?

Islands, therefore, can be places of challenge where you must learn to survive, fending for yourself on limited resources, or places of isolation and retreat where you dream about the good life – and listen to your desert island discs!

In each book of the series the author's purpose is to explore the uniqueness of a particular island and to convey the special appeal of the island. There is no common approach but in every case the island can be seen as a system in which a society is linked to its physical environment. An island culture can show clearly how the natural environment influences the ways people make a living. It also shows how people learn to modify or change that environment to make life better or more secure. This is very much a geographical view of islands, but the ideas and study skills used in the books are not limited to those of the geographer. The one controlling idea of the series is that islands are special places; small enough to know well and varied enough to illustrate the rich diversity of environments and lifestyles from all parts of the world. Islands can be places of social experiment or strategic importance, of simple survival or extravagance. Islands are the world in miniature.

John Bentley
Series editor

For details of other books in the Islands series, please write to Dryad Press Limited, 8 Cavendish Square, London W1M 0AJ.

Contents

ACKNOWLEDGMENTS

My special thanks to the Publishers for giving me the opportunity to write this book, and in particular to Ruth Taylor and Sandra Winfield for their editorial advice and assistance. Thanks too, to the Series Editor, John Bentley, for his help and encouragement.

All illustrations are by the author, except Figures 22, 25, 43, 44, 49 and 50, which are reproduced courtesy of the Spanish National Tourist Board, and Figure 65 which is courtesy of Mr. S. Robertson.

Cover photographs
The photographs on the front cover show gerias on the slopes of the Corona volcano; a local catch of octopus; the coast near Puerto del Carmen; and a beach at Playa de los Pocillos. The photographs on the back cover show salt pans on the island of Graciosa, and volcanic heat in the "Fire Mountains".

Typeset by Tek-Art Ltd, Kent
and printed and bound in Great Britain by
Richard Clay Ltd,
Chichester, Sussex
for the publishers Dryad Press Limited,
8 Cavendish Square, London W1M 0AJ

ISBN 0 8521 9727 6

LANZAROTE—PLACES & ROADS

SEE INSET

ALEGRANZA

Roque del Oeste

MONTAÑA CLARA

Roque del Este

GRACIOSA

GRACIOSA
Pedro Barba
Caleta del Sebo
Orzola
Bateria
Yé
Haria
Arrieta
Mala
La Costa
Caleta de la Villa
La Santa
Sóo
Los Valles
Guatiza
Tinajo
Tiagua
Teguise
Mancha Blanca
Mozaga
Tahiche
TIMANFAYA
San Bartolomé
Costa Teguise
El Golfo
PORT
ARRECIFE
Tias
Macher
Playa Honda
Yaiza
Uga
AIRPORT
Janubio
Femés
Playa Quemada
Puerto del Carmen
Playa Blanca

Km
0   5   10

1

Introducing Lanzarote

As the plane descends to Lanzarote's airport near Arrecife, passengers are treated to a remarkable bird's-eye view of the island's unique landscape. Many of those seeing it for the first time are tourists, and they might well wonder whether they have made the right decision in choosing this island as a holiday destination. The tourist magazines had said it would be different from most holiday islands, and they also warned that, on first sight, Lanzarote would seem strange, mysterious and even eerie. But did they say that the island's surface was like that of another planet, or like pictures taken of the surface of the moon? Do people really live on this lunar-like island of gaping craters, rugged lava fields and barren-looking areas of grey-black cinders? Those who arrive by ship might have the same feelings, although from the sea the craters are seen as mountain cones that look like large blisters and giant boils on a brown and parched landscape.

1 Lanzarote has a very rugged coastline, especially where the sea has carved caves into the volcanic lava. The volcanic cones in the background are between 200 and 400 metres high.

Whether arriving by ship or by air, the visitor will quickly realize that Lanzarote is a volcanic island. Its size, shape and character are largely the result of many violent and destructive eruptions. Some of these took place millions of years ago, but the island's most spectacular scenery is the product of volcanic activity during the last 250 years. Lanzarote's eruptions have left the island with a wild and rugged landscape in which there are some 300 volcanic cones of various shapes and sizes. Lanzarote is not volcanically dead, for close beneath its surface lies molten rock (*magma*) which could explode at any time. This is why the Spanish call it *Isla del Fuego* – "Fire Island".

There are others who would call Lanzarote *uno isla desierta* ("a desert island") for, as we shall see, it receives very little rainfall and has a severe water shortage. The island has, however, long been occupied by farmers and fishers. In fact, first-time visitors, disturbed by Lanzarote's appearance, will be relieved to see large inland villages of gleaming whitewashed houses surrounded by fields of crops. Many other settlements are scattered around the coasts, and some of these are now fast-growing tourist centres. The chapters that follow will explain how this dry, volcanic island manages to support a population of over 50,000 people, a figure which excludes the many thousands of holidaymakers who arrive every year. The story of Lanzarote is the story of the way in which its inhabitants have successfully tamed a wild, difficult and dangerous environment. This, as we shall see, has not been an easy task.

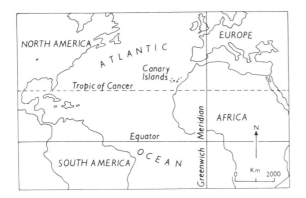

2 The geographical position of the Canary Islands.

3 Although Spanish, the Canaries are a long way from the Spanish mainland. Their Atlantic position, however, has always been very important to sailors. Today the main Canary ports are used by large ships on journeys between Europe, South America, the Indian Ocean and Australia. Las Palmas is Spain's largest international port.

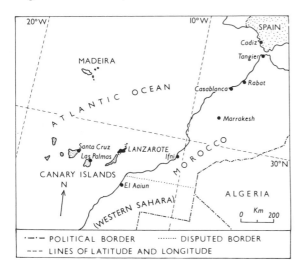

·—·— POLITICAL BORDER   ········· DISPUTED BORDER
—— — LINES OF LATITUDE AND LONGITUDE

Where is "Fire Island"?

Lanzarote is one of the seven main islands that make up the Spanish archipelago known as the Canaries, or Canary Islands. This group is situated in the eastern part of the Atlantic Ocean, to the south of Madeira and to the west of the southern coast of Morocco. The islands lie between latitudes 27°37' and 29°22' north, and longitudes 13°26' and 18°07' west. As

these co-ordinates show, the archipelago has a much greater east-west spread than north-south spread, and this accounts for important climate differences between the islands. The islands are only a few degrees to the north of the Tropic of Cancer, at a similar latitude to northern Florida, on the opposite side of the Atlantic.

Figure 4 shows the arrangement of the archipelago in more detail. As you can see, not only is Lanzarote the most northerly island of the group, it is also the most easterly; yet it is not the nearest island to the African mainland. The shortest sea-crossing from Africa is between Cape Juby in southern Morocco and Punta de la Entallada on Fuerteventura's south-east coast. This is a distance of 96 km. In contrast, Hierro lies a further 400 km into the Atlantic. As we shall see in Chapter 2, the geographical position of the Canaries was very important to sailors during the Great Age of Discovery.

Geographical differences

Look at the Table (page 7). It shows that there are big differences in the sizes of the seven islands, and also in their populations. Tenerife has the largest land area, but Gran Canaria has the biggest population. The figure of 836 sq km includes the areas of some smaller islands that belong to Lanzarote. These are Graciosa (27 sq km), Alegranza (10 sq km) and Montaña Clara (1.75 sq km) (see map on page 4). In addition there are the two rocky islets of Roque del Este

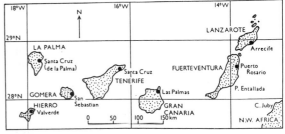

4 The geographical arrangement of the Canaries. The map gives the names of the seven main islands and of their capital towns or cities.

		Land area (sq km)	Population	Highest point (metres)
Province of Santa Cruz de Tenerife	Hierro	278	7,278	1,521
	La Palma	728	80,219	2,401
	Gomera	378	24,270	1,341
	Tenerife	2,058	585,815	3,718
Province of Las Palmas de Gran Canaria	Gran Canaria	1,558	591,445	1,965
	Fuerteventura	1,725	24,663	844
	Lanzarote	836	51,271	684

The land areas, populations and highest points of the Canary Islands

and Roque del Oeste (0.25 sq km between them). From these figures you should be able to calculate the area of Lanzarote itself. Of the smaller islands, only Graciosa and Alegranza are inhabited. The others are too wild and too dangerous to get to. Roque del Oeste is also called *Roque del Infierno* – "Rock of Hell", because many ships have been lost on the treacherous reefs that surround it.

The island's topography

The main part of Lanzarote is roughly oval in shape (Figure 5), with two narrower extensions, one in the north-east and one in the south-west. The island's width varies between 6 and 21 km, its narrowest part lying between Bahía de Penedo and Playa de la Garita. Lanzarote's maximum length is 60 km from Punta Fariones in the north-east to Punta Papagayo in the south-west.

The island has a very irregular coastline, whose total length is 169 km. Much of the northern coast is rugged, and parts of it have very high cliffs. The southern coast is gentler and here most of the island's sandy beaches are found. This area also has more settlements, including the port-city of Arrecife (the island's capital) and the main tourist resorts.

Look at the Table again. It shows that there are big differences in altitude on the seven islands. Lanzarote is, in fact, the least rugged and mountainous of the Canaries. The highest land is found in the Famara area in the north-east where some of the island's oldest rocks

are found (see Figure 18). Famara is really a ridge whose steep cliffs rise abruptly from the Atlantic. The main summits are Peñas del Chache (684 m), Volcán Corona (609 m) and Risco de Las Nieves (608 m). The eastern

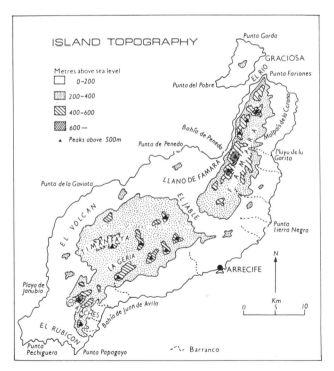

5 Lanzarote's topography. The Spanish name punta *is a common one around the island's coast. What do you think it means? Some* puntas *have lighthouses on them, so this should give you a clue. Together with the many bays* (bahías) *and beaches* (playas), *the* puntas *give the island a very irregular coastline.*

7

slopes of Famara are cut by a number of short, steep stream courses, but these are usually dry for most of the year. Any water that does flow in them is usually flood water. This causes a lot of erosion damage (see Chapter 5), leaving the small gullies full of boulders and other loose material. In Spanish, these dry, unstable stream courses are known as *barrancos*. As Figure 5 shows, all of Lanzarote's *barrancos* are found in the eastern and southern parts of the island.

In the south-west, Los Ajaches is another area where older volcanic rocks cause higher altitudes. Here Atalaya de Femés reaches 608 m and Hacha Grande 560 m. Los Ajaches is joined to the rugged centre of the island where the most recent (youngest) volcanic rocks are found. This area is divided into a number of districts – El Volćan, La Geria and Timanfaya; the last of these is also known as Las Montañas de Fuego ("The Fire Mountains") and is now a national park (see Chapter 12). Here there are numerous volcanic cones, many of them over 500 m high. The island's cones are discussed in more detail in Chapter 4, as are the large areas of barren, volcanic material which the islanders call *malpaíses*.

Most of the lowland areas are near the coast, but many of them are either too dry or too rugged for farming purposes, for example, El Rubicon, Malpaís de La Corona and parts of the Llano de Famara. This latter area, together with

6   The village of Haria, in the north of the island, is surrounded by rich farmlands. Behind it is the large Corona volcano, 609 metres high.

The Canary Island Provinces

As the Table on page 7 shows, the Canaries are divided into two Spanish provinces. This means that they are not colonies (as Gibraltar and the Falkland Islands are colonies of Britain), but an integral part of Spain. Along with Gran Canaria and Fuerteventura, Lanzarote belongs to the province of Las Palmas de Gran Canaria. The other four islands – Tenerife, La Palma, Gomera and Hierro – form the province of Santa Cruz de Tenerife.

How do you think the Canaries came to belong to Spain? You can check your ideas with the answers given in Chapter 2.

Lanzarote's population is growing rapidly and is now well over 50,000, more than half of whom live in and around Arrecife. The other important settlements are the tourist complexes and a number of small towns and large villages which are the centres of the island's municipalities (see Chapter 2). These have populations of between 2000 and 6000 inhabitants.

From the information given in the Table on land areas and populations, can you work out the population density for each island? In which position does Lanzarote come?

El Jable, separates the Famara ridge from the island's central volcanic region.

The "conejos"

The official name for the islanders is *lanzaroteños*, but they are more commonly known as *conejos* ("rabbits"), and the island is often called *conejera* ("rabbit warren"). No one is certain why these names are given. Is it because of the physical nature of the island? Or is it because of the special way in which Lanzarote is farmed? Perhaps it is because on many occasions the islanders were forced to shelter in caves from natural disasters or pirate raids from the sea. As you read through the following chapters, form your own ideas on this subject.

2

Exploration and conquest

The Canaries were known to seafarers long before the Spanish settled there in the fifteenth century. Unfortunately, much of what is said about them is mysterious, and most of the stories are now regarded as myth and legend. The ancient Greek writers talked about *Elysium*, a kind of paradise where heroes were sent after death to enjoy everlasting happiness. *Elysium* was said to be on the western edge of the world, beyond the Pillars of Hercules (Straits of Gibraltar). It was a land where "winter was unknown", and this is certainly a good description of the climate of the Canary Islands. The Greek historian Herodotus spoke of the *Garden of the Hesperides*, and this might also have been a reference to the islands. "Hesperides" means "in the west" and the garden was said to lie "at the edge of the world, where the sea could no longer be sailed". Another Greek author, Plutarch, talked of islands off Africa's north-west coast where "the breezes of springtime never stop". If you look through modern holiday brochures you will see that the Canaries are still referred to as "islands of eternal spring".

Probably the most famous legend associated with the Canaries is that of *Atlantis*, the large island in the "western sea" that was, according to Plato, destroyed by earthquake and volcanic activity. Plato also describes it as an *Utopia*, and many people have drawn maps showing where they thought Atlantis was located. Figure 7 is one of these early maps. On it the positions of the Azores (A), Madeira (M) and the Canaries (C) have been added. You can see that the Canaries are a long way from the

supposed edge of Atlantis. Although, as Chapter 3 explains, the position of some of the Canaries has altered during geological times, there is no evidence to suggest that they were once part of a much larger island. In fact, there is no real proof that Atlantis ever existed. If it did, then the recent discoveries of archaeologists suggest that it was probably located somewhere in the seas around southern Greece.

Carthaginians and Romans

The Phoenician sailors and traders of Carthage made many expeditions along the north-west coast of Africa. They came in search of natural dyes for their clothes and carpets and these were found on Lanzarote (see page 44) and the other islands. They called the Canaries the "Purple Islands", as this was the colour of the

7 *The supposed position of Atlantis. This old map was drawn according to the description Plato gives of Atlantis. The writing on the map says that the island of Atlantis is surrounded by sea to the west of Egypt (North Africa).*

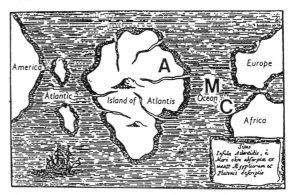

dye extracted from the orchil lichen and from a certain species of mollusc found around the shores of the islands.

Pliny the Elder, the Roman scholar, gives the first written account of the Canaries. He describes an expedition (about AD 30) sent by King Juba II of Mauritania – now Morocco. Juba's army probably landed on Lanzarote (or Fuerteventura) and though they found the remains of buildings, they saw no people, only large, wild dogs. One theory states that the name of the islands comes from these dogs, that is, from the Latin word *canis* ("dog"). So the Spanish name *Islas Canarias* means "Islands of Dogs". It is not true that they are named after the canary bird (*Serinus canaria*). Although native to the archipelago, the canary was imported into Europe in the sixteenth century, and the bird is named after the island, not vice versa. But, there is another theory which says that the name "Canaries" comes from *Chernes*. This is what the archipelago was called by its native peoples, and the word might refer to a species of fish, probably cod.

Who were the native islanders?

Although Juba's army saw no sign of human life, the islands were definitely inhabited at this time. The name now given to the original islanders is *Guanches*, but who they were and where they came from are questions that have still not been properly answered. Studies made of bones, pottery and rock drawings suggest that the Guanches were originally related to the prehistoric *Cro Magnon* peoples who lived in Southern Europe and North Africa at a time when the more northern lands were still covered with ice. These people could have reached Lanzarote and Fuerteventura when land bridges joined these "islands" to the African mainland (see Chapter 3). But the other view is that, guided by the winds and the sea currents (see Figures 29 and 33), they crossed over from Africa in simple boats at around 2000 BC.

European sailors and traders, many centuries later, described the Guanches as a

The Physical Appearance of the Guanches

The reports and diaries of the European sailors tell us what the Guanches looked like. They were quite tall and had light-coloured eyes and hair. This is how they were described: "You would have to travel all over the world before you would find a more handsome people, both men and women. They also have good minds, if anyone took the trouble to educate them."

The detailed account of the islands in 1590 by the Italian engineer, Torriani (who built the San Gabriel fort at Arrecife), also gives drawings of local Guanche costumes. The most common garments for men were animal skins, and the women wore dresses made of vegetable fibres, but these costumes were the result of European influence. Earlier accounts, such as that by Niccolosa da Recco, describe how many islanders went naked.

The Guanches liked to tattoo their bodies. Tattoos were described as "emblems cut on their flesh in different ways". Tattooing was (and still is) fashionable with the Berber people of North Africa, and some scholars believe that the Berbers and Guanches were related to each other.

8 *Some of the Guanche costumes shown by Torriani.*

people still living in the Stone Age. They lived in caves and rock shelters, made tools and weapons out of stone, and wore jewellery of wooden, bone and shell beads. They lived by hunting, herding sheep and goats, and a simple form of cultivation.

What was the reason for their archaic technology? It can be explained partly by the isolation of the islands, even those closest to Africa. Although it was quite easy to reach the islands in small boats, the direction of the winds and sea currents would have made the return journey to Africa or the Mediterranean very difficult. They were, however, able to cross from one island to another.

But the Guanches were not savages. In fact, they were a highly organized people. The natives of Lanzarote called their island *Titeroyugatra* and each large community had its headman who was responsible to the island's chief or "king". In the early part of the fifteenth century Lanzarote's "king" was called Guardarfia. Other important people were the priests and priestesses, as the islanders worshipped many gods. Their holy places were the high peaks and other natural features, especially the "Fire Mountains".

Insula Lanzarotus

Lanzarote and Fuerteventura were often raided by Arab and Berber pirates from Africa, probably in search of slaves. But to most Europeans this part of the Atlantic was known as the "Sea of Darkness". Although Lanzarote was the closest of the Canaries to Europe, it was not until 1336 that it was fully explored by the Genoese merchant sailor, Lancelotto Malocello. He sailed from Lisbon, as his voyage was financed by the Portuguese king. The Guanches welcomed Malocello to Lanzarote and he later returned to live there for twenty years. He ruled the island in the name of Portugal, and it is from this time that Lanzarote got its name – *Insula Lanzarotus*. This was the Latin name meaning "Island of Lancelotto".

Another expedition left Lisbon for the Canaries in 1341. Its leader was Niccolosa da

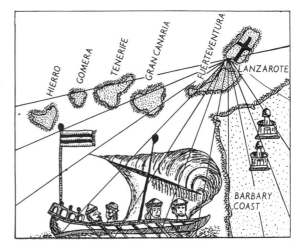

9 *The Canaries, as shown on the "Catalan Atlas" (1375). The Barbary Coast takes its name from the Berber tribes who lived there. By this time North Africa had been conquered by the Arabs, and its religion was Islam. What do you think the two peculiar-looking buildings are? Note how compass directions are taken from Lanzarote's most southerly point, Punta Papagayo. The map shows only six Canary Islands. Which one is missing?*

Recco, and again the islanders gave these sailors a friendly welcome. An account of this expedition survives, and Lanzarote is described as "a mass of uncultivated stony land, full of goats and other beasts". As a result of these sea contacts, the Canary Islands began to appear on maps. Figure 9 is a sketch taken from the "Catalan Atlas" (1375). You will notice that Lancelotto's coat of arms still covers Lanzarote, although he was probably dead by this time.

The Spanish Conquest

From the fourteenth century onwards Spain was the big naval and commercial rival of Portugal. Recognizing the important trading position of the Canaries, Spain decided to take the islands for herself. The conquest began in 1402 with the arrival on Lanzarote of Jean de Béthencourt (Figure 10). With him came his lieutenant, Gadifer de la Salle, two priests (who also acted as chroniclers) and an army of 250

10　Jean de Béthencourt was a Norman nobleman in the service of the King of Castille. He is regarded as the first real conqueror of the Canary Islands.

11　The village of Yaiza is the centre of one of Lanzarote's seven municipalities. Like all old island villages it is built around a central church and square.

men. The army was not needed as the islanders offered no resistance. In fact, they helped to build the fort in the Rubicon area in the south of the island, and this became a base for the conquest of the rest of the Canaries. Béthencourt needed more men to take the other islands, and when he returned to Spain for reinforcements trouble broke out on Lanzarote. The islanders, however, were quickly subdued, their lands seized and many became slaves. The Spanish forced them to accept the Christian religion, and even Guardarfia was baptised. Such methods of control were later used by the Spanish *conquistadores* in other parts of the world, especially in Central and South America.

When Béthencourt returned to Lanzarote in 1404 the island was made the seat of the first Catholic bishop in the Canaries. It also became the *Isla Senoriale* – the main centre of government. Béthencourt's nephew, Maciot, became Lanzarote's local ruler, and he was followed by Diego de Herrera, who built a new capital at Teguise. This was a safe inland position, away from coastal attacks, and Teguise remained the island's capital until it was replaced by Arrecife in the eighteenth century.

A part of Spain

The other Canary Islands were not as easy to conquer as Lanzarote. In fact, it took the best part of the fifteenth century for the Spanish to complete the task. In addition to subduing the Guanches, the Spanish had to deal with the Portuguese who still claimed the islands, especially Lanzarote. In 1470 Portugal gave up its rights to the islands to King Ferdinand and Queen Isabella of Castille and Aragon, and when Tenerife was finally taken in 1496 the entire archipelago became Spanish.

Four years before this final battle, Christopher Columbus, financed by Ferdinand and Isabella, had sailed from Gomera on his first voyage of discovery to the New World. Up until this time it was thought that Hierro marked the western edge of the world. Medieval geographers had placed 0° longitude at Hierro's western headland, Punta Orchilla.

With the discovery of the Americas the Canaries became a crucial trading post in Spanish colonial expansion. They acted as the geographical bridge between the Old World and the New. Following Spanish conquests in Central and Southern America, products from these areas were sent to Europe via the Canaries. The islands now attracted many thousands of Spanish settlers who came to farm, to trade and to build cities and ports. The Guanches were quickly outnumbered. Many had already been shipped to the New World as slaves, and the women who were left married into Spanish families. The original natives were almost completely wiped out. Yet, today, there is still evidence of Guanche blood in the large number of blue-eyed and fair-haired Canary islanders.

Pirates and forts

Because of the important trading position of the Canaries, France, England and Holland were also keen to conquer them. Pirates and privateers from these countries threatened the rich cargoes that were arriving from the New World. As well as this, Lanzarote and

12   Arrecife's fort of San Gabriel is joined to the city by a fortified bridge.

13   The church of San Miguel occupies the centre of Teguise, Lanzarote's old capital.

Fuerteventura were frequently attacked by raiders from North Africa. To defend the islands, Spain built a series of strong fortresses along the coasts and also at a number of inland positions. The sixteenth-century Guanapay fortress was built to protect Lanzarote's capital, Teguise, following an attack on the island by French pirates. The port of Teguise was Arrecife, which was protected by the fortress of San Gabriel (Figures 12 and 14). In the eighteenth century another fort, San José, was built to the north-west, near what is today Arrecife's new port.

Arrecife could not compete with the trade that went to Las Palmas on Gran Canaria or Santa Cruz on Tenerife. These were far richer islands whose wetter climates favoured the growth of many profitable New World crops. In the eighteenth and nineteenth centuries dry Lanzarote also suffered from natural disasters.

14   Plan of Arrecife. Arrecife is the Spanish word for "reef". This refers to the natural barrier of islets (in Spanish islotes) *that protects the city and its old harbour – Charco de San Gines. These islets are now connected either to each other or to the mainland by causeways. The fortress of San Gabriel is linked to the city by a stone drawbridge – Puente de las Bolas. The old part of Arrecife is located around the church of San Gines. Surrounding it are the new quarters and housing estates, or urbanizaciónes (see Chapter 10).*

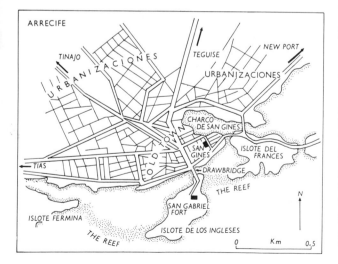

As we shall see in the next chapter, there were violent volcanic eruptions which devastated large areas of the island.

Modern developments

In 1821 the seven islands were made a Spanish province, whose capital was Santa Cruz on Tenerife. In 1852 the ports of this province were declared "open" or "duty-free", and they have remained the same up to the present day. This proved to be a very important step for island trade, especially when Spain lost many of her New World colonies in the Spanish-American War of 1898. The Canary ports continued to prosper and in 1927 two separate provinces were created (see page 8). Today the main island ports are visited by ships and tankers from Europe and America that must sail around Africa because they are too large to use the Suez Canal. What sort of cargo and destination are these ships likely to have? Why do you think they need to call at Canary Island ports?

The most recent development has been the creation of the Canary Islands as one of Spain's autonomous regions. This means they are now self-governing, but still part of the Kingdom of Spain. In addition, each island has its own local government – *Cabildo Insular.* Lanzarote's Cabildo is at Arrecife, and it has representatives from the island's seven municipalities – Arrecife, Haria, San Bartolemé, Teguise, Tias, Tinajo and Yaiza.

The Canaries are a long way from the Spanish mainland, which the islanders call the *Península* (its people are known as *peninsulares*). Cadiz is the nearest mainland port. Refer back to Figure 1. How far is Cadiz from the islands? What do you think are the main problems caused by this distance? Many *peninsulares* visit the Canaries for holidays, and many more come from other European countries, especially Britain, Germany and Scandinavia. They are attracted by the sun, sea, scenery and the duty-free status of the islands. They are the new *conquistadores.*

3

How the island was formed

To understand the way Lanzarote was formed, we have to look at the origins of the Canary Islands as a group. The archipelago has a complicated geological history, and there is still a lot of argument as to how it was formed. At present, the islands are the subject of detailed scientific investigation. This is taking place on both their land areas and in the seas surrounding them. Important new techniques include *radiometric* and *palaeomagnetic* surveys.

All seven islands have one thing in common – their surfaces are made up of rocks and other materials that are of volcanic origin. Many of these rocks are millions of years old; others are extremely new, for some of the islands still have volcanoes that emit periodic eruptions of lava. The most recent Canary eruption was in the southern part of La Palma in 1971. The great volcanic peak of Mount Teide (3,718 m) on Tenerife last erupted in 1909, and today it still smoulders. Lanzarote's last eruption was in 1824 but, as we shall see in Chapter 4, that part of the island known as the "Fire Mountains" is anything but extinct.

The "continental" theory

One of the main theories on the origin of the Canaries states that they were once joined to Africa, perhaps as a great headland or promontory. At some time in the geological past they became separated from the continent, and also from each other. If this theory is correct, then the islands belong to the type called *continental*.

It is important to remember that the real edges of continents are not their coastlines. Around the continents there are usually gently sloping, relatively shallow *continental shelves*. These extend some way under the sea before dropping steeply to the *ocean deeps*. Continental islands are those found on continental shelves. They are geologically linked to the neighbouring land mass from which they separated either when the sea level rose, or when there was a fall in the level of the land.

Look at Figure 15. It shows the continental

15 Plates and continental shelves. The boundaries of three of the earth's main plates meet in the North Atlantic. On either side of the Mid-Atlantic Ridge the American Plate and the Eurasian and African Plates are moving apart. The Eurasian and African Plates are moving together, that is, meeting head-on in a collision course.

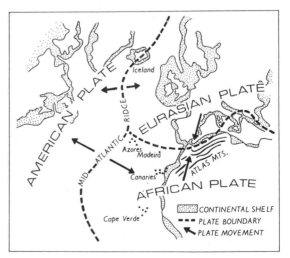

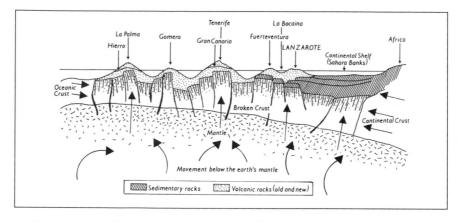

The geological structure of the Canary Islands.

16 *The geological structure of the Canary Islands. Sedimentary rocks belonging to the African mainland stretch under Lanzarote and Fuerteventura. In this part of the Atlantic the eastward movement of the Eurasian and African Plates (the Oceanic Crust on the diagram) is being halted by the force of the Continental Crust (where the Eurasian and African Plates are colliding). This movement of the three plates causes great fractures in the earth's surface, which extend down into the earth's mantle. It is through these fractures that magma rises to the earth's surface, causing volcanic eruptions on the islands.*

shelves around the western coasts of Europe and Africa. As you can see, the British Isles and some of the islands in the Mediterranean are of the continental type. What about the Canaries? Would you say that the entire archipelago is made up of continental islands? Refer also to the cross-section (Figure 16) and look at the way the non-volcanic, *sedimentary* rocks of Africa stretch under the sea to form the base rocks of Lanzarote and Fuerteventura. Do the other Canaries have similar structural links with Africa?

You would be right to say that only Lanzarote and Fuerteventura appear to be continental islands, that is, extensions of the African mainland. Only a narrow channel, the Sahara Banks, separates them from Africa's coast. Like the two islands, this channel stretches in a north-east to south-west direction. It was probably a great river valley before it was flooded by the Atlantic. It is also thought that Lanzarote and Fuerteventura were once a single island, and the same flooding led to the formation of the shallow channel, La Bocaina,

which now separates them. The bones of African animals have been found on Lanzarote, and one of the most interesting discoveries has been that of fossil ostrich eggs. How does this support the theory that there was once a land bridge between the two eastern islands and Africa?

The "oceanic" theory

Whereas Lanzarote and Fuerteventura can be regarded as continental islands, it is now believed that the rest of the Canaries are of the *oceanic* type. This means that they rose independently from the floor of the ocean, and are not extensions of the continental land mass of Africa.

Many of the world's oceanic islands are the summits of large submarine volcanoes. They are often a long way from the coasts of continents, and are usually surrounded by wide stretches of deep ocean. In the northern Atlantic, the volcanic Azores and Iceland are oceanic islands that lie on, or very near to, the Mid-Atlantic Ridge (Figure 15). This is a great chain of submarine mountain ranges and deep chasms that runs down the centre of the Atlantic. It marks the junction of some of the huge sections, or *plates*, that geologists now think make up the earth's crust. These plates are moving slowly in various directions. Some are moving away from each other, and some towards each other – on a collision course. The movements of these plates are the cause of such things as earthquakes, volcanic eruptions and the very slow building of mountain ranges.

On either side of of the Mid-Atlantic Ridge

Sea-Floor Spreading

The numbers given on this diagram are rough guides to the ages of the materials that make up the oceanic crust of the Atlantic. Because of sea-floor spreading, the youngest rocks are found around the Mid-Atlantic Ridge itself. But further away, in both directions, the rocks increase in age. Look at the position of the Canary Islands on this diagram. What are the ages of the basaltic rocks that underlie them? At one time these rocks were far nearer to the Mid-Atlantic Ridge.

How do scientists give dates to these rocks? One method is to measure the radioactivity that is present in all rocks. The amount of radioactivity decays (decreases) at a constant rate, which can be measured. Rocks, therefore, have their own "time ruler" by which they can be dated. Rocks also have magnetic particles in them, and these can also be studied and measured to indicate their ages.

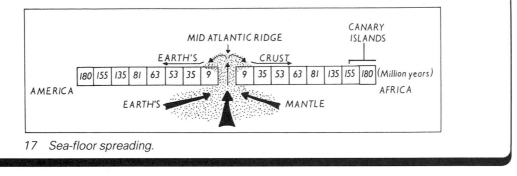

17   Sea-floor spreading.

the American Plate and the Eurasian and African Plates are moving apart. In other words, the Americas, and Europe and Africa, are moving away from each other. This movement is caused by the molten rock (*magma*) of the earth's mantle that constantly wells up through the great cracks along the Mid-Atlantic Ridge. This material is *basalt*, and it cools to form new ocean crust on either side of the Ridge, driving the plates apart. This process, which also happens in other parts of the world, is called *sea-floor spreading*.

Sea-floor spreading takes place very slowly. It is estimated that it would take one million years for the Atlantic to widen by 40 km (25 miles). If this is so, by how much does the Atlantic widen each year? This calculation is easy if you remember that 40 km represents 40 million millimetres.

If new crustal rocks are being added to the earth's crust, why isn't the earth growing in size? The answer is that equal amounts of crustal rocks are being destroyed. This happens in a *subduction zone* where plates collide and, especially, where one plate overrides another. When this occurs the edge of the lower plate is returned into the earth's

mantle where it melts and becomes part of the molten rock again. In other words the earth remains the same size because there is a balance between crustal rocks that are being formed and crustal rocks that are being destroyed.

What makes the Canaries volcanic?

Sea-floor spreading is the reason why the old rocks under the western Canaries are now far away from the area that produced them. Look at Figure 17. Some 155-180 million years ago the rocks were new crustal materials forming around the Mid-Atlantic Ridge. As more magma escaped and solidified, so the "Canaries" were gradually edged eastwards to their present position. They are still drifting slowly, but in this part of the eastern Atlantic there are other strong plate movements at work.

As Figure 15 shows, rather than moving apart, the African and Eurasian plates are colliding. This has led to the building of the great mountain ranges of southern Europe and north-west Africa – the Alps, Pyrenees, Apennines and Atlas, etc. These powerful forces of plate collision act as a brake to the widening of the Atlantic. This means that, in a similar way to the Mid-Atlantic Ridge, the area around the Canaries is another zone of weakness in the earth's crust.

The Atlas mountain ranges stretch in the same north-east to south-west direction as Lanzarote and Fuerteventura and the sea channel which separates them from Africa. In fact, the main *structural axis* of the Atlas extends under the Canaries, and Figure 18 shows how it runs through the centre of Lanzarote. Because of the forces caused by the colliding plates, the rocks beneath the islands are broken by large faults and fractures (see Figure 16) and it is through these, from time to time, that magma escapes to the surface. This is when volcanic eruptions occur.

This volcanic activity is largely responsible for the present size, shape and character of Lanzarote. The island's surface geology is shown in Figure 18. You can see how the older volcanic rocks have been covered by later ones, and there are also large areas of new, "historic", lavas. These recent eruptions and the landforms they have produced are discussed in the next chapter.

18　Lanzarote's surface rocks. The island's "historic" lavas are those from the eruptions of 1730-36 and 1824. The younger volcanic rocks shown on the map are a few thousand years old. The middle-aged rocks are around 5 million years old. The island's oldest rocks are between 5 and 20 million years old. The structural axis shows the continuation of the Atlas Mountains into the island. ▼

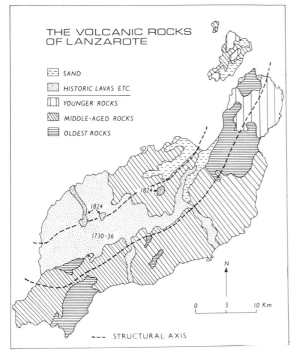

▲　20　El Golfo is an old volcanic crater which has been flooded by the sea. Its sides are made of different layers of lava.

19　The wild and weird-shaped rocks along ▶ Lanzarote's west coast were formed when molten lava cooled on reaching the sea.

4

Lanzarote landforms

Volcanic regions are said to be *active* when eruptions are actually taking place. Most eruptions last for short periods only, a few days, a few months, or a year or two at most. Between eruptions volcanoes usually remain *dormant* for much longer periods, amounting to several years, or even several hundred years.

Lanzarote's volcanoes have been dormant for over 150 years, but they could easily become active again. There is plenty of evidence of there being intense heat only a short distance below parts of the island's surface. In the "Fire Mountains" temperatures reach 100°C a few centimetres below ground level, and at a depth of a few metres temperatures of 400°C have been recorded. Dry twigs dropped into holes quickly burst into flames, and water poured into pipes set upright in the ground is rapidly changed to powerful geysers of steam. Even cigarettes can be lit, potatoes baked and eggs fried. In fact, the high temperatures of the "Fire Mountains" are harnessed in a kitchen and restaurant where visitors can eat food cooked by the volcanic heat itself. For the islanders, therefore, the expression "living on top of a volcano" (that is, "living dangerously") has very real meaning.

21 In parts of the "Fire Mountains" steam and volcanic gases escape from the hot ground below.

The historic eruptions

Refer back to Figure 18. It shows the areas covered by the lavas and other materials from the island's last two eruptions. Over 200 sq km, about one quarter of Lanzarote's surface, were affected. These eruptions took place in 1730-36 and in 1824. For both of them we have eye-witness accounts.

The 1730-36 period of activity gave rise to thirty new volcanic cones. On and off, the eruptions lasted for nearly seven years, making this one of the world's longest periods of volcanic activity. In fact, it was said that many of the *conejos* came to accept the dangers as an inevitable part of their daily lives. But the damage caused was very great. Some of the island's richest farming land was ruined and eleven villages, including Maretas, Tingafa, Vegas de Timanfaya, Santa Catalina and Jaretas, were destroyed. As new volcanic vents opened up, the islanders were forced to flee for their lives. Some hid in sea caves, or in old volcanic caverns away from the main danger areas. Others crossed over to Fuerteventura, or left the Canary Islands for good.

This is how Don Andres Curbelo, who lived near the village of Yaiza, described one of the eruptions:

"... the island trembled. This was the most violent of the earthquakes that had been rocking it. The earth suddenly opened near Timanfaya, two leagues from Yaiza. Steam began to escape from the ground and this was followed by a rain of cinders and fine ash. Darkness was caused by the ash and smoke that filled the sky and covered the island. Lava poured out like water and flowed towards the north. Soon its speed slackened and it flowed like honey. The lava quickly destroyed the valley villages of Maretas and Santa Catalina. This was not the first time that the people of Yaiza had fled for their lives. They saw new cones growing among older cones. Then a stream of lava issued from a new cone and flowed towards Jaretas. It set the village on fire and destroyed the church of St. John the Baptist near Yaiza. . ."

This is a very full account of the order of events that come with most big volcanic eruptions. What was the first thing that happened to the ground? Why do you think the lava's "speed slackened" and it began to flow "like honey"? Make a list of the other things that came out of the new volcanic vents.

Some of the ejected materials Curbelo mentions are known as *pyroclasts*. This is the name given to smaller pieces of solidified lava that, depending on their size, are scattered over wide areas. When lava reaches the surface the gases in it expand and shatter it into molten pieces which quickly harden as they fall to the ground. The largest of these *pyroclast* pieces are the *volcanic bombs* which vary in size from a few centimetres in diameter to several decimetres. In 1730-36 they caused much damage as they fell on the island's villages and farmlands. Smaller rock fragments, about the size of a pea or hazel nut, are known as *lapilli* or *volcanic cinders*. Then there are the finest particles, the *volcanic ash* and *dust*, which are often carried long distances by the wind. As we shall see in Chapter 7, the islanders make great use of the *pyroclast* materials, especially the *lapilli*.

Compared with the eruptions of 1730-36, those of 1824 were less violent and there was far less damage. They lasted for just a few months and only three new volcanic cones were formed. The smaller areas involved are shown on Figure 18. But there were some spectacular results, especially where the lava from the main eruption reached the sea, producing scalding sea-water sprays. Similar scalding sprays were also common during the 1730-36 eruptions. Where do you think they occurred? Refer to Figure 18 again.

22 These volcanic cones, formed by the eruptions of 1730-36, are part of the Timanfaya National Park. ▶

The volcanic cones

The most obvious landforms of Lanzarote are the *volcanic cones* and their *craters*. There are over three hundred of them, and only the largest are shown on Figure 23. Many of the old cones have a greenish colour which is caused by *lichens* that grow on their surfaces. The 33 new cones (from the last two eruptions) have very little plant life on their slopes. Their grey-black, red-brown and yellow-orange colours are those of the volcanic materials that form them.

Most of the island's cones are of the *composite* type. This means that they are made of various layers of lava and pyroclasts that collected around their vents during eruptions. Some of the smaller cones are almost perfectly conical in shape, but the majority, especially the larger ones, have

23   Lanzarote landforms. Note how the main volcanic cones follow the north-east to south-west structural axis. A similar straight alignment of cones is shown on Figure 22. Why do you think the cones take on this particular pattern or arrangement?

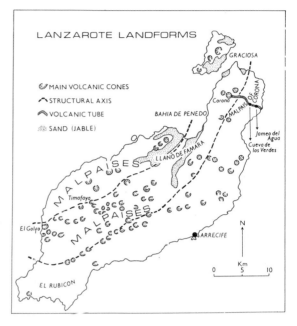

24   These diagrams show some typical Lanzarote cones. What has caused the irregular shapes of A and B? Look carefully at diagram C which shows a small regular-shaped cone and a larger irregular one. Both are shown to be erupting, the ejected materials being the finer pyroclasts. What explanation does the diagram give for their different shapes?

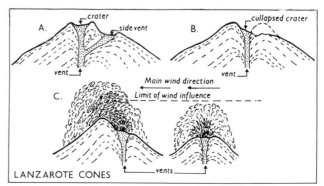

irregular profiles. Many things explain the differences in size and shape — how long the eruptions lasted, the type of material ejected, and the number of vents from which the material came. Many of the large volcanoes have a main vent and one or more smaller or subsidiary vents. On some cones the crater has collapsed to produce even more irregular profiles. The islanders, too, have altered the shapes of cones by using them as quarries for building-stone or for *lapilli* which they use on their fields.

The malpaíses

As well as escaping from vents and cones, the lava from Lanzarote's eruptions streamed out of *fissures*, or cracks in the island's surface. How far it travelled depended on whether it was the thicker *acid lava* or the more liquid *basic lava*. The former covered only short distances, as it flowed slowly and cooled quickly; the latter travelled long distances before cooling and becoming solid. Another factor that controlled the flow of lava was the slope of the ground. As noted, some flows reached the sea where they formed rugged cliffs.

25 A "camel-train" in the "Fire Mountains". The animals are crossing an area of loose volcanic material. In the centre of the picture is an area of malpaís, and beyond are high volcanic peaks.

Many of the island's lava flows are up to ten metres thick. They form very difficult, untamed landscapes which the islanders call *malpaíses*, that is, "badlands". Large areas of "badlands" surround the main volcanic cones of the "Fire Mountains" (see Figure 23) and another area, the Malpaís of Corona, is found in the north. Look at the rugged area of lava shown in the central part of Figure 25. What are the main difficulties caused by such areas? Certainly they are almost impossible to cross and, as you can see, even the Lanzarote camels have to keep to the easier ground.

Like the volcanic cones, the "badlands" of the "Fire Mountains" have hardly any vegetation, for the lava has not yet weathered to produce a soil cover. The Malpaís of Corona is an area of older lava flows, but it too supports only a vegetation of lichens and sparse succulent plants. As you would expect, the "badlands" are useless for either cultivation or grazing purposes.

But the "badlands" are of great geological interest. They show many complicated lava patterns. It is important to remember that the surface of a lava stream, because of contact with the air, cools and solidifies more quickly than the central flow. This means that when the surface hardens, the molten material beneath continues to flow until it also begins to harden. This was the main cause of the ripples, swellings, cracks and weird shapes that can be seen today. Many of the holes in the lava surface are old bubbles formed by escaping gases. Other features are the huge rock balls found on and around the lava flows. These were produced when molten material on steep slopes broke away from the front of the main flows. As they cascaded down, they hardened to form large jagged balls which came to rest where the slopes were less steep. As well as lava, the "badlands" have large areas of pyroclast materials.

Volcanic caves

Large underground caves are found in the Lanzarote lavas. Some were caused by

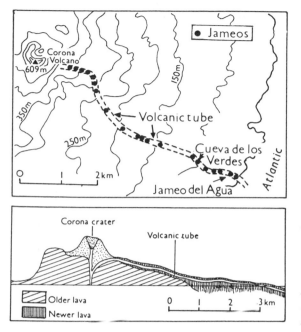

explosive gases, and others by the build-up of steam which also blew openings in the solidifying rocks. But the most impressive caves are found in the island's north, in the lava stream that once flowed from the Corona volcano to the sea. These caves are part of a 6 km-long *volcanic tube* whose twisting course (Figure 26) marks a depression in the ground which was probably an old *barranco* course. The line of surface holes, or *jameos*, was formed when parts of the tube's roof collapsed.

26   *The Corona volcanic tube. The line of surface holes, or* jameos, *was formed when parts of the tube's roof collapsed.* Cueva de los Verdes *(the "Cave of Greens") takes its name from the multi-coloured lavas, many of which are shades of green.* Jameo del Agua *means "Waterhole", so called because it contains the remnants of old sea-water pools.*

The Formation of a Volcanic Tube

From the three diagrams, can you work out how a volcanic tube is formed? Remember what has been said about the behaviour of lava flows – when the surface of the lava stream solidifies, cooled by contact with the air, the liquid material underneath continues to flow.

Diagram 1 shows a stream of lava flowing from a volcano. In diagram 2 the volcano is still erupting, but the outer layer of the lava has crusted over. Underneath, however, the lava continues to flow. In diagram 3 the eruption has stopped, and by this time most of the lava has drained out of the tube.

As you would expect, some lava also solidifies in the tube and is the cause of its rugged floor and sides. Within the tube there is usually a series of caves or galleries, some often at different levels. In time parts of the roof will collapse to form the surface *jameos*.

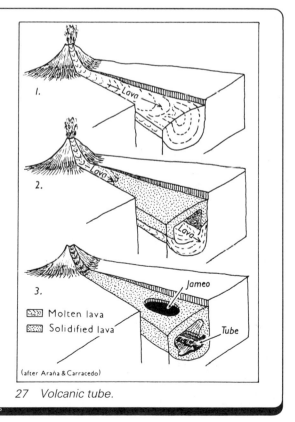

(after Araña & Carracedo)

27   *Volcanic tube.*

It is possible to visit two large complexes in this volcanic tube, and both are now big tourist attractions. Cueva de los Verdes is a series of rugged galleries and caverns, parts of which are still unexplored. One section is called El Refugio, an old hiding-place of the Guanches, and also in later times when the islanders were plagued by pirate raids. At the seaward end of the tube is the other cavern area open to visitors. (In fact, it has been turned into a nightclub.) This, the Jameo del Agua, was also the result of a massive steam explosion when the lava in the tube reached the sea. Some of the water that once filled the huge caverns remains as a dark salt-water pool, the habitat of a unique species of white, blind crab.

Erosion

The rugged scenery of Lanzarote is also a result of the way the volcanic landforms are being eroded, or worn down. Lanzarote is a windy island (see chapter 5) and, armed with fine rock particles, the wind cuts weird shapes in the exposed volcanic rocks. Material is also blown about to form volcanic dunes. The camel train in Figure 25 is crossing such an area of dunes, whose surface is made of loose pyroclast materials.

The grey-black colour of these volcanic dunes is very different from that of the island's other sand areas – the light-coloured *jables*. Look at Figure 23 to see where these are located. The large Bay of Penedo (Bahía de Penedo) is a stormy part of the island's coast. Here the waves are constantly attacking the steep cliffs of the Famara, and the eroded materials are carried by the strong northerly winds to form large areas of sand, especially in the lowland area at the head of the bay, the Llano de Famara. In this area, and also on Graciosa, some of the sand has consolidated to form sand wastes. These are partly colonized by vegetation and provide poor grazing areas suitable only for goats.

The sea is responsible for many impressive landforms, especially where volcanic cones have been attacked by the waves. An example is El Golfo (see Figure 20), an old cone whose seaward side has collapsed. Its crater has been flooded to form a volcanic lagoon, and the work of the sea has also revealed the many shapes and colours of the volcanic materials that form this cone. Refer back to Figure 24. Do you think you should include the work of the sea as another important cause of the irregular profiles of Lanzarote's volcanoes?

28   *A local fisherman tries his luck off rocks at Punta de Penedo.*

5

A desert island

When the Romans called the Canaries the "Fortunate Islands" they were really referring to Gran Canaria and the islands in the western part of the archipelago, especially Tenerife. Along with Fuerteventura, Lanzarote is the least "fortunate" of the group, for not only is it volcanic, it is also extremely dry and has a severe water problem. Lanzarote, in fact, has the lowest rainfall total of all the Canary Islands.

Geographical position

The differences in climate between the islands can be explained partly by the closeness of the eastern islands to the North African coast and partly by the oceanic position of the western islands, which extend for some 500 km into the Atlantic. As you can see from Figure 29, Fuerteventura and Lanzarote lie off the shores of the Saharan desert, which is shown by the Subtropical dry climatic belt. Generally speaking, those islands closest to Africa are hot and dry, those farthest away are more temperate and receive more rainfall. This means that the western islands have climates similar to the Mediterranean area shown on Figure 29, and they grow a rich variety of crops, including bananas. One main reason for the greater rainfall in the western islands is the presence of peaks and mountain ranges that are high enough to intercept the moisture-bearing winds.

29 African climatic belts and the Canaries Current. The Sahara Desert is marked by the Subtropical dry climatic belt. This is further divided into semi-arid and arid zones, the latter being the true desert.
The Canaries Current cools the seas around the Canary Islands.

Lanzarote's rainfall

Deserts are usually regarded as those parts of the world that have less than 300 mm (12 inches) of rainfall a year. Figure 30 shows the monthly average rainfall totals for Arrecife.

30 Can you work out the average yearly rainfall total (in mm) for Arrecife? Is this amount more or less than the amount given for a desert area?

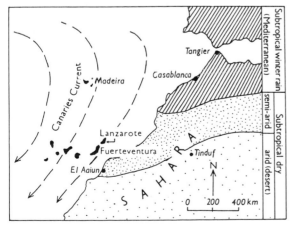

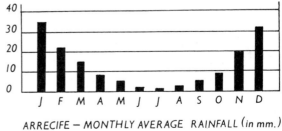

ARRECIFE — MONTHLY AVERAGE RAINFALL (in mm.)

*31   Lanzarote's annual rainfall distribution. Can you ▶
suggest why there is more rainfall in the north-west
and in the centre of the island? To help you explain
this pattern refer back to Figure 5. Are there any
parts of the island with an annual rainfall total higher
than the total given for a desert climate?*

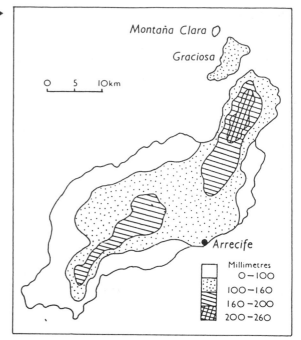

Which are the four wettest months? As you
can see, the rest of the year has much smaller
amounts and in summer there is hardly any
rainfall at all. But, as in deserts, when rain does
occur, it usually comes in very heavy showers,
often thunderstorms, and these cause a lot of
damage. For a short time the island's *barrancos*
fill with water, and soil, boulders and other
materials are washed into the sea.

It is important to remember that Arrecife is
situated on the coast, and that some parts of
Lanzarote receive higher rainfall totals (Figure
31). Another point to note is that the rainfall
figures given for Arrecife are annual averages

▲
*32   A satellite picture of the cloud front of the Trade
Winds as they approach the Canaries.*

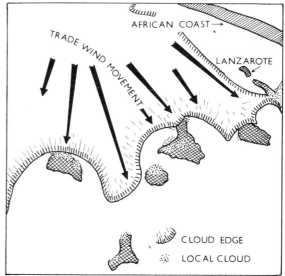

▲
*33   The Trade Winds approaching the Canaries.
The diagram helps to explain the photograph, and
Lanzarote has been marked on it. Can you recognise
the outlines of the other islands? In the top right
corner the African coast is also shown. The dark area
is space, beyond the earth's curvature.*

for a 20-year period. In actual fact, monthly and annual totals vary greatly from year to year. Some years are wetter than others, but it is not uncommon for Lanzarote to experience droughts lasting up to three years.

The Trade Winds

Much of the Canaries' rainfall is brought by the North-East Trade Winds. Where these blow over land they are usually "dry", that is, they bring little or no rain. But where they blow over oceans they absorb much moisture. This means that the *relative humidity* of the air around the Canaries is usually very high, and on Lanzarote it can reach 70 per cent. In order for rain to occur, some mechanism, or "trigger", is needed which forces the moist air to rise. When air arises, it cools, and because it is then unable to hold as much moisture, rainfall occurs. One of the ways in which air is made to

34   From what is said about orographical rainfall in this chapter, can you explain the rain-making process over the Famara? What do you understand by the term rain-shadow? This northern part of Lanzarote has the island's richest natural vegetation cover. Some of the plants, especially those growing on the steep sea cliffs, are rare species.

rise is when mountains stand in its path. This type of rainfall, the most common in the Canaries, is called *orographical* or *relief* rainfall.

Figure 32 is a view from space of the great belt of cloud that marks the North-East Trades as they blow towards the Canaries. You can see how the islands interrupt the south-westerly path of the Trades, forcing the air to move between, and over, the islands in a scalloped pattern. As the air rises, *condensation* takes place and *orographical* rain falls on many of the northern and western slopes. Some of the islands' highest summits, however, also have their own local cloud cover. But look how the cloud belt completely misses Lanzarote. This is what happens for most of the year, for the island is on the eastern edge of this Trade Wind system, and much of Lanzarote is also too low to intercept the Trade Wind moisture. The Famara area, however, is high enough to receive regular orographical rainfall and some orographical rain, though less frequently, falls in the centre of the island.

Island temperatures

The average monthly sea and air temperatures for Arrecife are shown in Figure 35. In graph B both the average monthly minimum and the

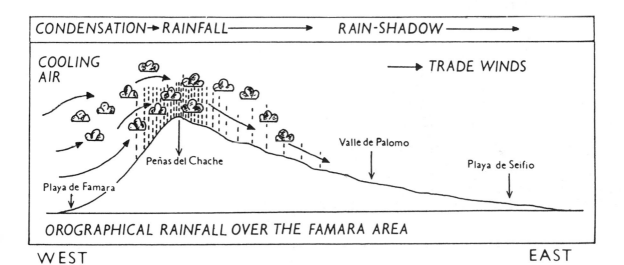

CONDENSATION→RAINFALL—————→   RAIN-SHADOW—————→

COOLING AIR   ——→ TRADE WINDS

Peñas del Chache

Valle de Palomo

Playa de Seifio

Playa de Famara

OROGRAPHICAL RAINFALL OVER THE FAMARA AREA

WEST   EAST

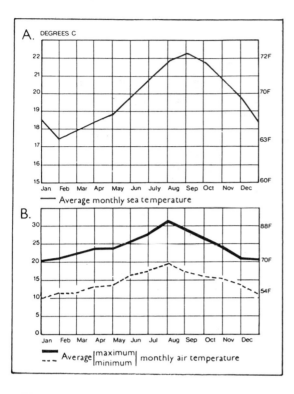

A.

DEGREES C

— Average monthly sea temperature

B.

— Average |maximum / minimum| monthly air temperature

35 *Average monthly air and sea temperatures for Arrecife. Which months have the coolest air temperatures, and which month has the hottest? Do the coolest and hottest sea temperatures occur in the same months as the coolest and hottest air temperatures?*

average monthly maximum air temperature are recorded. Again, it is important to remember that these figures are averages. Temperatures can fall below the minimum, and rise above the maximum values given for each month. For example, August temperatures can sometimes reach 37°C (100°F).

In general, Lanzarote's air temperatures are lower than we would expect considering the island's latitude. The main reasons for this are the influence of the surrounding sea and the cooling effects of the Trade Winds. But another important factor is the Canaries Current (see Figure 29), a "cold water" current urged equator-wards by the Trade Winds. Any good atlas will have a map showing ocean currents. Can you find cold currents in other parts of the world that are similar in location to the Canaries Current?

Because of the cooler seas around Lanzarote, low cloud or coastal fog is common. But this rarely lasts for long as the winds are usually strong enough to mix the air and disperse the fog. Late winter and early spring is generally the foggiest period. You can see from graph B that this is when sea temperatures are lowest. Even so, the island's sea temperatures are still high enough for people to enjoy bathing and water sports throughout the year. This helps to explain the island's fast-growing tourist industry.

Land and sea breezes

Study the temperature graphs again. You will see that the warmest and coolest temperatures for the air and sea do not occur in the same months. This four-week "lag" is caused by the different behaviour of solids and liquids to heating and cooling. Which do you

Xerophytes

Most of the wild plants of Lanzarote are *xerophytes* – those that are adapted and able to survive in dry areas. The most common *xerophytes* found on the island are the *succulents*, plants that are able to store moisture in their fleshy parts. The many varieties of local *cactus* belong to the succulent family. Cacti have tough, swollen stems and their leaves have been reduced to prickly spines or scales. This greatly reduces the amount of *transpiration*, by which a plant loses moisture.

Other plants on the island need careful tending and watering, especially the many ornamental plants that are not natives to Lanzarote. Most come from the wetter Canary Islands. The gardens, patios and balconies of village homes, modern apartments and new hotels have many flowering shrubs and potted plants. Great favourites with the islanders are the geranium, hibiscus and bougainvillea.

think heats up, and cools down the quicker, the land or the sea?

As well as occurring seasonally, the same process takes place on a daily-nightly basis. During the day the land heats up more quickly than the sea, and at night it also cools more quickly. This causes air pressure differences which lead to *land and sea breezes*, also known as *diurnal winds*.

Lanzarote's winds, both seasonal and diurnal, can be very strong, and they can do great damage to soils and young plants. They also increase *evaporation* and *transpiration* rates, and this causes further moisture problems. As we shall see, the islanders have devised many ways of protecting their crops from the strong winds.

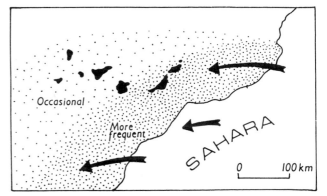

SAHARAN DUST OVER THE CANARIES

37 *Saharan dust. Dust blown from the Sahara Desert is more common in the eastern than in the western islands. As they are further out in the Atlantic, the western islands have only occasional dust storms.*

The approach of the dust is a spectacular sight. The blue sky gradually turns red-brown, and this is a warning for the islanders to take precautions.

Saharan dust

As well as the main seasonal and daily winds, Lanzarote also receives winds that blow out of the Sahara (see Figure 37). Fortunately, they are not very common, and rarely do they blow for more than a few days. The Saharan winds are dry and usually carry particles of fine dust and sand which get everywhere. The streets of Arrecife and those of the island's villages become coated with a thin layer of this powder. It also gets into the eyes, hair and nostrils, and even into the works of watches and cameras. All food and drinking water have to be covered. The only people to get some benefit from these winds are the farmers, for the dust provides a useful addition to the island's soils.

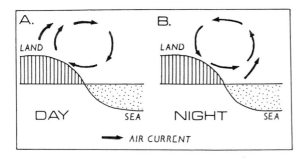

36 *Land and sea breezes. During the day, the warmer air over the land rises to form an area of relatively low pressure. This attracts winds that blow in from the sea – on-shore winds. At night, the reverse process takes place; the land cools more quickly and air is drawn away from the land towards the sea, which is now warmer and, therefore, the area of lower pressure. These are known as off-shore winds.*

These changes mean that Lanzarote has big temperature differences between day and night. This is especially the case in summer, when the absence of cloud means that there is nothing to stop the land heat escaping into the atmosphere. Hot days and chilly, often very cold, nights are characteristics of desert and semi-desert climates.

6

The water problem

The shortage of water has always been a major problem on Lanzarote. Today it is an even bigger worry, because extra supplies are needed as more and more tourists visit the island and others come to live permanently. Now, Lanzarote's water needs are far greater than those that the island can provide. The water supply comes from both surface and underground sources, but together they meet only half of the island's needs.

The search for new water resources is going on all the time. Some improvement has come from the building of desalination plants, but quantities of fresh water are still brought in by tanker from Gran Canaria and Tenerife. Yet, in spite of their higher rainfalls, these islands have their own water problems. This means that, in the future, Lanzarote cannot expect to rely on water brought in from outside.

In Arrecife and the holiday resorts the water is perfectly safe to drink, but it is not particularly pleasant. This is because it is desalinated sea water to which chlorine has been added. For drinking, many islanders, and especially visitors, use bottled water sold in shops and supermarkets. This is relatively expensive, for it, too, is imported from other Canary Islands and parts of mainland Spain. Imagine what it would be like if you had to buy drinking water every day. You would certainly appreciate the value of water much more and be careful not to waste it.

38 The distribution of Lanzarote's main water ▶
sources. The area that shows where water vapour reaches the surface is the fumarole region of the "Fire Mountains".

Surface supplies

We have already seen that Lanzarote's annual rainfall is both small and variable. Much of the rain that does fall in a year is quickly lost by evaporation, run-off or by filtering into the dry ground. Over 70 per cent of the island's rainfall is lost in these ways. One of the main concerns of the *conejos*, therefore, is to collect and store as much water as possible.

Look carefully at Figure 38. This sketch is a summary of some of the main sources of Canary Island water. Can you distinguish between surface sources and underground sources? Lanzarote uses most of these methods of obtaining water, but some are far

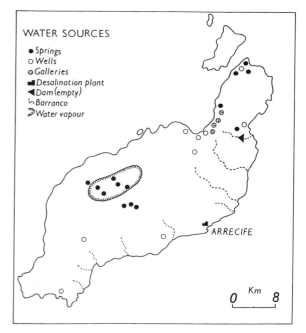

WATER SOURCES
- ● Springs
- ○ Wells
- ⊚ Galleries
- ◼ Desalination plant
- ◀ Dam (empty)
- Barranco
- Water vapour

ARRECIFE

0   Km   8

which is measured by a monitoring device. The water is either stored in tanks or conveyed in pipes and canals to farms, fields and villages. As galleries are difficult and costly to build, a new one can only be justified if there is some guarantee of a good supply of water. On Lanzarote no source of water is certain to last for any length of time.

Other water sources

As well as the island's main desalination plant at Arrecife, some of Lanzarote's large new hotels also have their own plants for removing salt from sea water. With hundreds of guests at any one time, hotels and tourist villages need a very great amount of water. What do you think uses the most water in hotels? Remember, too, that a lot of water is also needed for the grounds and gardens that surround the tourist complexes.

Desalination plants are costly and on Lanzarote they depend on imported oil. Experiments are under way on the use of alternative sources of power, such as the wind, the sea and the volcanic or *geothermal* heat of the "Fire Mountains".

The "Fire Mountains" are also a source of water. Figure 38 shows a group of springs located in or near to what is a *fumarole* region. Fumaroles are openings in the ground through which steam (and other gases) escapes from the magma below. On reaching the surface the steam condenses to form springs, which can be recognized easily by the small patches of vegetation that grow around them. But, at present, these springs are wasted, and the water is quickly lost because of the porous volcanic materials and the high ground temperatures. The steam needs to be piped, as this would lead to its condensation, and the water could then be distributed to villages and farmlands.

Lanzarote's local council (*Cabildo*), and also the Canary Islands' government, is very interested in the ways in which other dry areas of the world are tackling their water problems. For example, in Israel research has gone into new methods of desalination, the purification of stagnant water and artificial rain-making, etc. But Lanzarote is a small island with a small population. It could never afford such expensive schemes unless a great deal of money were invested in the island from outside. As we shall see in the next chapter, the islanders themselves are the main experimenters in finding and using new supplies of moisture.

7

How the island is farmed

With rain so rare, and underground water supplies limited, you might wonder how Lanzarote manages to be a farming island. In fact, it grows a variety of crops (see Chapter 8), and some of them are exported to neighbouring Canary Islands, to mainland Spain and to other European countries. How do these crops flourish under such dry conditions? What skills have the farmers developed to turn parts of the island into rich areas of cultivation? The islanders would answer that the secret lies in what they call "the miracle of the cinders". They would probably be too modest to add that the island has really been tamed by them, by their sheer hard work, experiment and inventiveness.

Dry farming

Few of the water sources shown in Figure 38 find their way to the island's farmlands. Hardly any of Lanzarote's fields are irrigated; rather, cultivation is by the *dry farming* method. This depends on catching what little moisture there is, and then storing it within reach of the roots of the plants that are grown. Dry farming means that land has to be prepared, or treated, to overcome the water shortage.

But water shortage is only one of the problems of the Lanzarote farmers. The farmer also needs a suitable soil cover. As we have seen, large parts of the island are covered with volcanic materials that have not yet weathered to produce soil. The lack of rainfall is partly the reason for this, for without adequate rainfall the natural vegetation is poor. Vegetation is vital to the formation of a soil, for it helps to provide the *humus* layer on which a soil's fertility depends. Without this layer a soil is said to be "undeveloped" or "immature". Yet, buried beneath many areas of volcanic material, "mature" soil does exist. Provided it can be uncovered, and receive moisture, crops can be grown.

The island's climate leads to other soil problems. High temperatures cause the rapid evaporation of moisture. This leaves layers of salts which gradually build up and make soils infertile. Then there are the steady winds, which dry out the soil further, and also cause the top layers to be blown away. The farmers have built wind-breaks and devised other forms of shelter for their fields and plants.

Fans and terraces

Some of the best of Lanzarote's farmlands are found around the villages of Los Valles and Haria, in the north of the island. Here the older rocks of the Famara have had time to weather and produce more mature soils, and, as noted, this part of the island also receives more rainfall. It is also the most mountainous part of Lanzarote, and the soil has been washed down from the steep slopes and has collected in the valley bottoms to form what are called *alluvial fans*. (Figure 42).

In order to increase the amount of agricultural land on some of the steep Famara slopes the farmers have built lines of cultivation terraces. These follow the contours of the hillsides and the step-terracing helps to stop

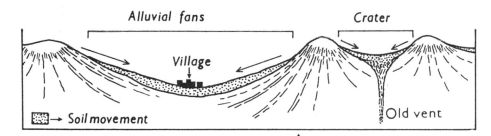

Alluvial fans

Crater

Village

Soil movement

Old vent

42 Forms of soil collection. The alluvial fans provide good areas for growing crops. Soil has also collected inside some of the craters of old volcanoes. The craters act as "reservoirs" that capture rainfall and they also provide protection from the wind.

The "Fertility" Monument

One man who has paid tribute to the farmers' success is César Manrique. He is the island's famous artist, architect and planner, and we shall learn more about his work in Chapter 10. To honour the farmers, Manrique has designed a piece of modern sculpture, that stands on a rocky outcrop near Mozaga, in the centre of the island. Called *Fecundidad* (which means "fertility" or "productiveness"), this 10-metre high monument is surrounded by vineyards and fields growing other crops. It is a symbol of the way in which the farmers have successfully cultivated their dry, volcanic lands. But, in fairness, it also honours the camel, for without this beast of burden the farmers' task would have been even more difficult.

43 Cultivation terraces in the Famara. The large fans are the result of storm water washing soil and other material down from the higher slopes.

41 The Fecundidad monument.

the loss of soil. Why do you think that plants with long roots, such as vines and figs, are grown at the front of these terraces? Behind them cereals and vegetables are grown, and these are further protected by *bards*. These are shown on Figures 44 and 45. The Haria area is also famous for its tall date palms. These, too, have long roots for tapping moisture at depth.

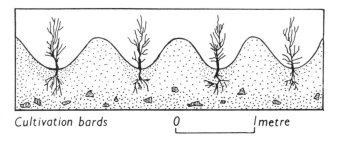

Cultivation bards

0   *Imetre*

▲
44 Bards *are deep field furrows made by the farmers to shelter young crops from the winds. They also help with the storage of moisture.*

The enarenados

As well as cultivating hill terraces and the insides of craters, the farmers grow crops in even more unusual ways. Visitors to the island will see specially prepared fields which have a cover of black volcanic material. These fields are called *enarenados* from the Spanish verb *enarenar*, which means to cover with sand. The "sand" the Lanzarote farmers use is the volcanic *lapilli* which they call *picón*. The best *picón* comes from only a few volcanic cones. Camels are still used to carry it to the fields, but now lorries are more common.

Look at Figure 46. It shows that an *enarenado* is like a big sandwich, made of different layers of material. Preparing it is a complicated business. First, the land is cleared of rugged lava stones, and these are used to

45 *Lanzarote women work hard in the fields. Here they are weeding bards. The large straw hats give them protection from the hot sun.*
▼

build wind-breaks around the edges of the fields. The ground is then ploughed or hoed, and covered with a layer of manure. Sometimes a thin layer of clay is also added, as this helps to retain the soil moisture. Finally, the entire field is covered with *picón* to a depth of 7 to 20 cm, depending on what crops are to be grown. Where the natural soil depth is shallow, extra supplies are brought from other parts of the island.

Why do the farmers take such trouble in preparing these fields? What is the purpose of the *picón*? Look at the Figure 46 again. Are the crops actually growing in the *picón*? One of the things the *picón* does is protect the valuable soil from blowing away. It also reduces the day-time evaporation of the moisture in the soil below. The *picón* contains a lot of silica, and this "glassy" mineral helps to reflect the sun's rays, shielding the soil from the high temperatures that would dry it out completely.

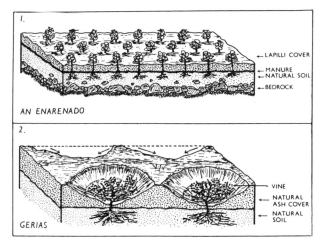

46 Enarenados and gerias. Enarenados are found on some of the other Canary Islands, especially Tenerife. Gerias, however, are special to Lanzarote. They are sometimes referred to as "flower-pot" cultivation.

The "miracle of the cinders"

The main advantage of the *picón* is the way in which it attracts and absorbs moisture from the atmosphere. One result of the island's nightly heat loss (see Chapter 5) is the dew that forms on cooler surfaces such as soils, plants and rocks. It is difficult to measure dew-fall, but it is said that Lanzarote's yearly total is about 25 mm. Although this is a small amount of moisture, it is vitally important to plant life, especially during the driest months. The *picón* acts like a big sponge and traps the nightly dew-fall essential to the nourishment of crops. In other words this volcanic cover becomes a moisture reservoir, and without it the farmers would find it impossible to grow many of their crops.

The man-made *enarenados* can last for up to twenty years, but they need to be regularly topped up with *picón*. In time the *picón* gradually gets mixed in with the soil, and when this happens it loses its sponge-like property, and crops begin to suffer. The farmer then has to start the whole process of making new fields again.

The gerias

Perhaps the most unusual Lanzarote method of growing crops is in *gerias*. These are funnel-shaped hollows in the ground up to 5 m in diameter. Some of the best examples are found in La Geria, a district in the west of the island named after them. La Geria is famous for its low-growing vines, whose bright green leaves contrast with the dark *picón* that surrounds them. Only the upper branches of the vines are visible, for the *gerias* slope down to 1.5 m below the surface.

The island has thousands of *gerias* and many are built along the lower slopes of volcanic cones, giving the landscape a scalloped effect. Some are the result of the farmers digging into the thick volcanic cover to reach the soil layer below. As Figure 46 shows, the vines (and other plants) grow in the soil, and the *picón* again acts as a moisture reservoir. Importantly, the hollow also protects the plants from the wind. Another trick the farmers have learned is to build walls of lava or, nowadays, concrete blocks around part of the *geria*. Standing in the path of the prevailing winds they provide extra

47 *Gerias on the lower slopes of the Corona volcano. Some of them are growing vines.*

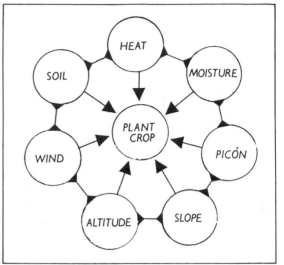

48 *A geria as an ecosystem.*

protection, and they also shield plants from the sun's rays for part of the day. The farmers have worked out that even one extra hour of direct sunshine each day would be enough to kill many plants in the *gerias*, especially the vines.

Man-made ecosystems

The farmers have made the *gerias* into self-contained *ecosystems* where there is a delicate link, or balance, between the plant and its local environment. Figure 48 shows the main factors that affect the plant's growth. However, this balance in the *geria* can be easily upset, and when this happens the plant suffers. All the factors are linked, and all are responsible for a healthy crop. Can you suggest ways in which the *ecosystem* balance might be upset and, as a result, the crops destroyed?

Farm tools and animals

Farming the island is obviously very hard work. The farmers are rarely away from their fields and plots. A common sight is a long line of workers, men and women, occupied in such jobs as hoeing, weeding, repairing walls and harvesting. Children also help in the fields, especially at harvest time.

Much of the work is done with simple hand tools such as shovels and hoes. On the larger fields the old stick-plough, or Roman plough, is still used. Figure 49 shows it being pulled by a camel, though sometimes a donkey and camel are yoked together. The donkey is a far less powerful animal, but it is easier for the farmer to control. When the donkey is made to move forward, stop and turn, the camel follows.

Lanzarote's Camels

Why do you think the camel is an important animal on Lanzarote? Some of the work it does is shown in Figure 49. This type of camel is the Arabian variety and is also known as the dromedary. It is found throughout the dry lands of North Africa and the Middle East.

The first camels were brought from Africa, probably in the fifteenth century. They quickly felt at home on the dry island and were used to work the land and as transport animals. The camel is an animal of great strength and can carry loads of up to 500 kilograms balanced on wooden W-shaped saddles. Camels are also used for threshing. Tethered to a threshing pan, the animal patiently moves in circles, gradually separating the grain from the chaff.

There used to be many more camels working the land. Their numbers have fallen since the introduction of tractors. But large parts of the island are not suited to agricultural machinery. Can you give reasons for this? Nowadays, camels which are no longer needed on the land have other tasks to perform. As Figure 50

49 Ploughing an enarenado. The woman is sowing grain seed. When fully ploughed the field will be covered with a layer of picón.

shows, they are used to carry visitors to the top of the "Fire Mountains" to which access would be otherwise difficult. These sure-footed animals are used to dry and rugged country, but their passengers are still given a bumpy ride!

50 Visitors to the "Fire Mountains". Camels take them to the tops of the volcanic peaks.

8

Products of the land

From the information given in the previous chapter, why do you think it is difficult to give an accurate figure for the amount of land that is cultivated on Lanzarote? Figure 51 shows those parts of the island where some form of crop growing takes place, but it gives only a very general picture of the cultivated land, for not every part of it is actually growing crops. As we have seen, the island's farm-land is in short supply, and those areas cultivated are intermixed with dry, barren lands. Many of the crops are grown in small and scattered fields and plots. For example, it is difficult to estimate the amount of crop-land in the hillside terraces. And what about the *gerias*? Refer back to Figures 43 and 47 and you will be reminded of the difficulty in measuring the amount of cultivated land on the island. The main areas of *gerias* are shown on Figure 51 by the distribution of vineyards.

The main crops

The Lanzarote farmers grow crops both for subsistence (that is, to feed themselves and their families) and for profit. The latter — the island's cash crops — are sold locally, or are exported to the Spanish mainland and other European countries. An important export crop is onions. The seedlings are planted by hand in neatly laid out rows in the *enarenados*. They grow into the big, firm and strong-tasting variety — onions found in British supermarkets with the "Produce of Spain" label may well have come from Lanzarote.

More recently, the growth in tourism has greatly increased the demand for local farm produce. The large hotels, restaurants and holiday villages need regular supplies of fruit and vegetables, and the farmers also sell to the supermarkets in Arrecife and elsewhere. But the best place to see the range of crops the island grows is in the old market in the centre of Arrecife. Depending on the season, early morning is the best time to view the stalls of

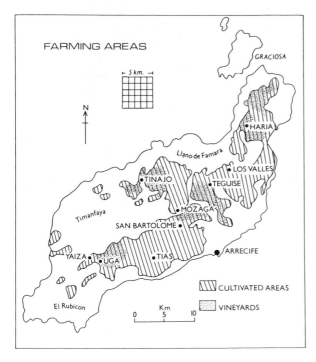

51 *Lanzarote's farming areas. By using the key you can measure the amount of land made up by the shaded areas. What proportion of the island's area does it represent? Remember that Lanzarote's total land area is 795 square kilometres.*

52 Tomatoes, onions and beans are the products sold on this stall in Arrecife market.

beans, potatoes, lentils, peas, melons, onions, garbanzos (chickpeas), sweet potatoes, corn-on-the-cob and carrots. In addition, the island grows cereals, figs, some tobacco and large amounts of juicy grapes that are used to make the famous Lanzarote wines.

Many farmers are now experimenting with growing tomatoes, a crop that has become profitable on Fuerteventura. Like all Lanzarote crops, tomatoes demand constant attention and a regular supply of moisture. As yet, most of the tomatoes sent from the Canaries to northern countries in winter and spring are mainly from Tenerife and Gran Canaria.

Wine

The way in which most of the island's vines are grown has already been explained. The vine stock is the type known as *Malvoise*. This is named after Monemvasia in southern Greece, from where the vines are said to have been brought to the Atlantic islands in the fifteenth century. The famous Malmsey wines produced from them were extremely popular in the royal courts of Western Europe. Shakespeare mentioned Malmsey, but he was probably referring to the wines of Madeira rather than to those of Lanzarote. The two are similar, however, and the Lanzarote variety is called *Malvasía* (see Figure 53).

Although they are no longer the mainstay of the island, grapes still remain an important crop. The grape harvest begins towards the end of August, when each well-tended vine can produce between 100 and 200 kg (220-440 lbs) of fruit. Camels can be seen patiently waiting between the *gerias* as their wooden panniers are filled with grapes for conveyance to the wine presses. Most farmers keep enough of their grape harvest for their own needs, and some of the old foot-pressing methods are still used. But most of the grapes go to the large modern wine-presses in Arrecife. *Malvasía* is considered to be one of the finest wines of the Canary Islands. It has a special quality and flavour that come from the island's volcanic soil and *picón* covering. Wine experts describe the *seco* variety as "rich, dry and fragrant, with a tang of acidity". There is also a sweet *Malvasía — dulce*. Both varieties have a high alcohol content — sometimes as much as 17 per cent. This strength is said to be the result of the small amount of moisture the grapes receive during growth. Like Madeira wine, the Spanish sherries and the ports of Portugal, *Malvasía* is usually served as an apéritif or an after-dinner drink.

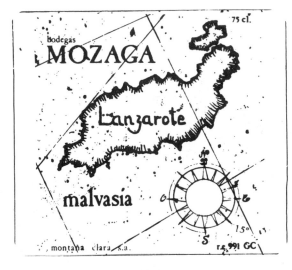

53 *Lanzarote wine label.*

In the past the Lanzarote vines suffered from diseases which frequently ruined harvests. Today, the big problem is competition from other wine-producing regions, especially on the Spanish mainland.

Cactus plantations

What do you think red-striped toothpaste, pink cake icing, *Campari*, lipstick and raspberry-coloured fizzy drinks have in common? The answer is that they all contain cochineal, a non-poisonous dye or colouring made from the crushed bodies of the *cochinella* insect (*Dactylopius coccus*). This was introduced to Lanzarote around 1825, and one story tells how the insects were brought from Costa Rica in a traveller's hollow walking-stick.

Cochineal production is another example of the unique ways in which the islanders have profited from their dry lands. The insect feeds on the *opuntia* or *nopal* cactus, and this was also brought from Central America. As it survives in areas of dry and infertile soils, it was a plant well suited to Lanzarote. Large *opuntia* plantations were created during the nineteenth century, and cochineal brought big profits at a time when there were few chemical or artificial dyes.

Island Dishes

The islanders enjoy many different meat dishes, and pork, lamb, chicken and rabbit are prepared in a variety of ways. Beef, however, is expensive, as it is imported, mainly from Brazil. Soups and stews, with plenty of vegetables, are specialities of the island. They are often eaten with *gofio*, once one of the mainstays of the Guanche diet. *Gofio* is made from grains which are first toasted before they are ground. It is then made into dumplings, or it can be eaten as a bread.

Many island dishes include *papas arrugadas* ("wrinkled potatoes"). These are small new potatoes cooked in their skins in sea- or salt-water. They are eaten with their skins on, and are usually accompanied by a hot sauce called *mojo*. This is made of oil, vinegar, salt, peppers and spices. *Mojo picón* has red peppers and is very hot; *mojo verde* (made with green peppers) is milder.

The islanders also prepare the more familiar Spanish dishes. These include *tortilla española* (omelette with potatoes, onions and other vegetables) and *gazpacho* (a cold soup make from tomatoes, onions, pimentos, olive oil and island wine). A favourite dish in all Spanish areas is *paella* – rice cooked with saffron in a large pan, to which meat, fish and vegetables are added. The *paellas* of Lanzarote contain more fish than meat.

▲
54   Most of the remaining cactus plantations for raising cochinella are in the north-west of the island, around the villages of Mala and Guatiza.

55   The cochinella thrive on the shaded sides of the opuntia leaves where they feed on the sap of this cactus.
▼

As we have seen, this was not the first dye to be collected on the island. The Carthaginians probably came to Lanzarote in search of the red-purple dye extracted from molluscs living around the coasts. Another natural dye was obtained from *orchil*, a member of the lichen family, that grows wild on the island's cliffs and volcanic slopes. Orchil dye was needed for Europe's textile industries, but because the lichen grew wild and could not be cultivated, it was quickly over-harvested. This led to the decline of the dye as an item of trade, as did the introduction of chemical dyes.

Lanzarote's cochineal production has also been affected by the general use of artificial dyes. Today, there are few new *opuntia* plantations, although *cochinella* are still raised around the villages of Mala and Guatiza in the island's north-east. Here, in spring, the fine eggs of the *cochinella* are introduced onto the shaded sides of *opuntia* leaves. When the eggs hatch the insects form colonies of grey-black bugs, about three millimetres long, and resembling small wood-lice. They feed on the sap in the cactus, and their bodies contain the substance that is the dye.

Harvesting is usually the work of women who scrape the mature insects into a can with a long-handled spoon. Up to three harvests, at about six-weekly intervals, can be made. After collection the insects have to be killed, otherwise their removal from the cactus food supply will lead to their eating each other. When they have dried in the sun they are sent to mills in Las Palmas to be processed into powder. Some cochineal is still used in the textile industry, especially as dye for carpets. But most of it is exported to the Spanish mainland, the United Kingdom, Japan and the USA where it is used in the manufacturing of cosmetic, food and drink, and pharmaceutical products.

Can you think of other things you eat and drink, take as medicine, or use in the bathroom that might contain cochineal colouring?

Livestock

Would you expect Lanzarote to have many domesticated farm animals? Look at the Table and compare the numbers of animals on Lanzarote with those found on the other Canary Islands. In particular, why do you think the island has so few cattle?

	Cattle	Sheep	Goats	Pigs
La Palma	2,242	712	16,423	6,751
Gomera	440	545	3,320	917
Hierro	650	1,300	2,160	375
Tenerife	8,057	1,831	33,932	11,862
Gran Canaria	17,569	8,327	68,480	22,125
Lanzarote	67	179	5,300	934
Fuerteventura	219	1,550	19,820	1,140

The numbers of farm animals on the seven islands

Many of the island's cattle, in fact, are oxen which are used to work the fields along with camels and donkeys. There is hardly any fresh supply of cow's milk. Most milk is tinned, powdered or the "long-life" variety imported from countries such as Holland. Much of the island's butter comes from Ireland.

As you can see, neither does Lanzarote have many sheep. These animals also need suitable pasture-lands and cannot survive on the island's rugged lava fields or areas of loose volcanic materials. Goats are different. They are foraging animals adapted to rough areas with poor vegetation. Herds are often seen clambering over the island's steep cliffs and slopes in search of food. They are highly destructive of the natural vegetation cover, for they eat most moisture-containing succulents, even the prickliest of cactus. Goats are kept for their meat and milk, and many farmers make goat's cheese (*queso blanca*). Pigs are found on most farms and pork is a common item on Lanzarote menus, as is locally cured ham. Other animal products come from chickens and wild rabbits. The latter are much used in traditional island stews.

56   Camels and donkeys are the working animals on most Lanzarote farms. They often feed on the husks of maize.

Goat's Cheese

White goat's cheese (*queso blanca de cabra*) was an important part of the diet of the Guanches. It is still made in villages all over the island, following a traditional recipe.

Preparation usually begins in the evening. The goat's milk is warmed to 25°C and 8 fluid ounces of fresh buttermilk are added for each quart of milk, together with a few drops of *rennet* diluted with 8 fluid ounces of water. The *rennet* is responsible for curdling the milk. The mixture is stirred well and the pan is then placed in a large box or basket lined with paper to keep the mixture warm. In some villages hay is used instead of paper.

By the next morning the milk should have curdled, and there should be some whey on the top of the mixture. The curd is then put into a cheese-cloth and hung up to drain for 6-12 hours at a temperature of about 20°C. When drained the curd is mixed with cooking salt and put into earthenware (nowadays plastic) moulds. The curd is pressed well to remove all the air. After a few hours the cheeses are taken out of the moulds and put in a cool place. Here they are left to ripen (mature). The longer they are left, the stronger their aroma and flavour.

9

Harvesting the sea

Because of the many difficulties in farming the island, the lanzaroteños also look to the sea as a means of livelihood. But although fish are an important part of the local diet, fishing has never played as important a role as agriculture in the island's economy. There are, however, a number of communities where fishing is the only occupation. Some of these date from the time when natural disasters ruined inland villages and farmlands. For many, the alternatives were to leave the island, or to move to the coast.

On Graciosa, the people of the two small hamlets of Caleta de Sebo and Pedro Barba depend almost entirely on the sea, and Lanzarote itself has many fishing villages scattered around its coasts. One of the most important is Caleta de la Villa on the Bay of Penedo. Here there are some large houses belonging to old fish merchants.

57 At Caleta de la Villa, small fishing boats lie in wait for their next trip to sea.

In-shore fishing

Fishing operates on two main levels. One of these, in-shore fishing, is purely local, and the other, off-shore fishing, is commercially organized from Arrecife. Small boats are used for in-shore fishing and the men work long, hard hours at sea, usually at night. In the morning the entire family (and friends) will be on the beach to help pull in the boats and assist with the catch. Children also have to work hard sorting the fish and washing out the boats.

The family has the first choice of the catch, and if it is a good one the rest is put on the beach to be weighed on home-made balances using stones as weights. The surplus is usually sold to hotels and restaurants, but some of it also goes to the island's canning factories. On occasions the catch is sufficiently large for quantities of fish, usually sardines, to be prepared for drying. These small fish are gutted

58 *Most of Lanzarote's off-shore fishing boats are old and poorly-equipped.*

and split open, and then sprinkled with salt before being laid out on wire racks to dry. Like most Canary islanders, the lanzaroteños enjoy dried raw fish as a snack or *tapas*.

Even if they don't own a boat many islanders spend their spare time with a fishing rod. They also contribute to the family diet by searching rock pools to see what fish have been stranded by the receding tide.

Off-shore fishing

The most important fishing waters are those that lie between Lanzarote (and Fuerteventura) and the north-west coast of Africa. This narrow stretch of ocean is part of the Sahara Banks, one of the eastern Atlantic's main fishing grounds. Most of the world's major fishing activities takes place on "banks", a word given to sections of continental shelves where, as we have seen, ocean water is shallower. Refer back to Chapter 3. What did it say about the stretch of water between Lanzarote and Africa? Look again at Figure 16. What does it tell you about the depth of the sea to the east of the island, compared with the depth of the sea around the more western Canaries?

Because of the relative shallowness of continental seas, the sun's rays penetrate far enough to encourage plant growth and, especially, *plankton* — small plant and animal particles that float in sea water. Both are important sources of fish food. The movement and mixing of waters of different temperatures and salinity is also important in supporting life. Look back to Figure 29. What does it show as being the main cause of water-mixing off this part of Africa's coast?

The Sahara Banks contain large shoals of both *demersal* fish (those living in deeper waters) and *pelagic* fish (those that occupy the upper or surface waters). Some of the *demersal* species found and caught around Lanzarote include cod, haddock, hake and plaice. The most important *pelagic* varieties (which the in-shore fishermen also catch) range in size from the small anchovy, sardine, herring and mackerel to the large tuna. Also caught are sea bream, squid, octopus, bonito (a type of tuna), shrimp, prawn, lobster, crab and a variety of shell-fish. The main game-fish, now an important tourist attraction, include barracuda, shark, sword-fish and tuna. The latter are the largest fish caught around Lanzarote, and they can be up to three metres in length and weigh 600 kg (1,300 lbs). Their favourite prey is herring and mackerel, whose migrations they follow.

Lanzarote's off-shore fishing fleet uses the harbours of Arrecife, which is one of the Canary Islands' main fishing ports, second only to Las Palmas. Most of the smaller vessels moor in the old inlet of Charco de San Ginés (the "pool" of San Ginés, so called because the town's main church overlooks it). Larger vessels use the new port that was opened in 1960 to the north-east of the town. In recent years, however, the volume of fish landed at Arrecife has greatly decreased and the fishing fleet is much reduced. Part of the reason for the smaller catch is the number of old and poorly-equipped vessels that are still in use. There is a need for modern refrigerated boats, that can fish further out to sea, and also for a general improvement in fishing techniques. In addition, the port's handling and warehousing facilities need modernizing. However, there have been important improvements in Arrecife's fish canning and preserving factories. This has led to a big increase in the export of processed fish such as tuna, anchovy, mackerel and sardines. The waste products are used for fish-meal and fertilizers.

Fishing conflicts

The seas around Lanzarote are now being over-fished. In addition to local Canary fleets, vessels from Morocco and from as far away as Norway, Russia and even Japan fish the Sahara banks. Many of these foreign vessels are "factory ships", on board which the fish are processed, usually to frozen fillets. The Canary fishermen greaty resent these fleets of other nations being close to their coasts.

The most serious conflicts over fishing rights in the Sahara Banks have occurred between Spain and Morocco, and there has been much argument between Madrid and Rabat over regulating fishing limits between the two countries. Morocco, however, demands an off-shore fishing right of some 110 km, that is, the right to fish most of the waters in this part of the Sahara Banks. Many Canary fishermen have experienced trouble from the Moroccan authorities, and some have even been taken hostage for "political reasons". It is important to remember that it is not just fishing that Morocco and Spain are arguing about — there might well be large deposits of oil beneath the Sahara Banks.

The salt industry

Extracting salt from the sea is an old Lanzarote industry. The traditional way of producing salt is to flood coastal hollows, or pans, and let the sun and wind evaporate the water. The island has many areas of salt pans, but the biggest are found along the El Rio coast in the north and at Salinas de Janubio on the south-west coast. Most of the salt is used in the fish factories, though some of it is refined for use as kitchen and table salt.

Janubio produces about 10,000 tonnes of salt a year. Here a large artificial lake has been created, and is divided into numerous square salt pans. Sea water is pumped into these pans, and left so that it gradually evaporates. After about four weeks the salt is removed and put into piles to await transport to the processing plants. The white pyramid shapes of the salt make an unusual picture, especially as the lake often has a turquoise-blue appearance. Janubio is a popular place for ornithologists as it is a haunt of resident water-fowl and migrant birds.

Some of the salt is used at the spring festival of Corpus Christi. Local artists dye the salt various colours, then use it to create religious and other pictures on the pavements and streets of Arrecife. The island's coloured volcanic sands are used for the same purpose. This type of street decoration also takes place on some of the other Canary Islands, but on Tenerife and Gran Canaria flowers are used instead of sand. From what you now know about Lanzarote's weather and climate, what would you say is one of the big problems these artists have in laying down sand pictures?

60   *The island's largest area of salt pans is at Janubio on the south-west coast.*

Sports – Old and New

Many sea-water activities, such as swimming, fishing and boating, come naturally to the islanders. Others, however, are new and have developed along with the tourist industry. There are also some traditional Canary Island sports which both fishermen and farmers enjoy.

One of the oldest sports found on Lanzarote and the other islands is Canary Wrestling (*Lucha Canaria*). It is said that the Guanches wrestled to strengthen their muscles and to quicken their reflexes. But wrestling matches were also the means of settling disputes, such as those over the ownership of land.

Wrestling matches are still popular on Lanzarote. Two teams of twelve wrestlers (*luchadores*) are involved, though only one wrestler from each side competes at a time. They fight barefoot and dress in a shirt and shorts. A special ring 9 metres in diameter is used, and its floor has a thick covering of sand. Each bout lasts for only a few minutes and the man whose body touches the ground first is the loser. The rules, however, are much more complicated than this, and there are some 24 wrestling "holds" and positions.

Another sport that has lasted through the centuries is *Juego de palo*. This is a kind of fencing match using long flexible sticks. As with wrestling, the rules of this game are passed on from father to son.

Although some island boys start to learn the arts of wrestling and fencing at an early age, most young people prefer the modern sports, especially football. This is Spain's national sport and most of Lanzarote's towns and villages have football teams and league matches. Being Spanish, some islanders are also fans of the bull-fight (*corrida de toros*), but there are many others who are not convinced that this is a sport. The nearest bull-ring that attracts famous *matadors* from the Spanish mainland is in Las Palmas.

Bowls (*bolas*), played in open places, is a popular game with men.

59   A local bowls match at Arrecife. This game is common to other parts of Spain and southern France.

Other sea resources

As we saw in Chapter 6, the sea also provides Lanzarote with drinking water and, in the future, it could be used as a source of energy. Today another new resource of the sea is the opportunity it provides for all sorts of leisure and sporting activities, such as swimming, sailing, wind-surfing, snorkeling, deep-sea fishing and water skiing. Of all the island's settlements, the coastal villages are changing the most, especially those close to safe, sandy beaches. Many are now fast-growing holiday centres and other coastal sites are marked for development, including the desert-like sandy beaches of Graciosa.

The resort villages

Lanzarote's first tourist villages were built in the south, where some of the island's best beaches (*playas*) are found. South-west of Arrecife, and close to the airport, are a number of resorts – Playa de los Pocillos, Playa Blanca and Puerto del Carmen. These have now grown to form a single tourist area of hotels, villas, apartments, restaurants, bars and boutiques. In the south is the fast-growing Playa Blanca (Sur). Like Puerto del Carmen, this is an old fishing village that has been transformed into a holiday and residential centre. To the north-east of Arrecife is the Costa Teguise, a resort area that has grown around a large, luxury hotel with huge landscaped gardens.

Because of its ruggedness and exposure to the Atlantic winds, the island's north coast is not such a popular tourist area. The exception is the Playa de Famara with its many holiday homes. Some of these are owned by the wealthy of Arrecife who are also buying homes in other new *urbanizaciónes* or "estates" (see Chapter 10). Close to the city is Playa Honda, a rapidly developing coastal suburb of expensive villas.

61 *The whitewashed houses of Uga contrast with the dark shades of the surrounding fields and volcanic mountains.*

10
Tourism and island planning

During the last fifteen years Lanzarote has seen a big increase in the number of tourists visiting the island. Tourism, in fact, is now the most important industry, and Lanzarote is the third most popular holiday destination in the Canaries, after Gran Canaria and Tenerife. In addition, many people arrive every year, especially from Britain, Germany and Spain, to buy villas or apartments on the island. Some of these are elderly people who come to the island to retire; others just want a holiday home, and a popular way of getting one is by the "Timeshare" method. From what you have read in the previous chapters, can you list some of the attractions Lanzarote can offer holiday-makers and those looking for a place to retire to?

62   *Many new hotels have been built in Arrecife, but the Gran Hotel is the island's only high-rise block.*

The effects of tourism

Tourism is now bringing a lot of money to the island, but it is an industry that is also causing rapid changes to the Lanzarote landscape and way of life. As more people come to the island, so more land is needed for development. Some islanders have benefited by selling land to the property developers, most of which are companies from the Spanish mainland and other European countries, especially Germany and Britain. *Wimpey*, the building firm, for example, is a well-known name on the island.

But the rapid and uncontrolled growth of tourism can also bring many problems to small island communities. How would you feel if foreign companies were to buy large areas of land in your village, town or neighbourhood, and then use it to build hotels, villas and apartments for overseas tourists? Would you want to see the place where you live advertised as a new resort in, say, French, German and Spanish holiday magazines? Some local people would certainly make money out of the tourists, and there would be many new jobs for builders, hotel staff and shopkeepers. But others in the local community might suffer, especially if the foreign tourists have plenty of money. This would mean that the prices of land, homes, food and other things would almost certainly rise. Imagine your neighbourhood full of German *Bierkellers*, Spanish *bodegas*, French *bistros* and nightclubs that are too expensive for your family to visit. How would you react to this situation?

This kind of tourist development has happened in many parts of the Canaries, including Lanzarote. But the island's *Cabildo* is now carefully controlling all new tourist schemes. It is particularly concerned that new buildings and facilities should be of the highest quality and not spoil the island's landscape and atmosphere. Even so, tourism is greatly altering Lanzarote. Figure 63 shows some of the advertisements that appear in English magazines sold on the island. Other foreign (that is, non-Spanish) magazines have similar

63 The effect of tourism on Lanzarote. Why not design your own poster for Lanzarote? There are many colour photographs in old holiday brochures you could use. Many newspapers also have advertisements and information on Lanzarote holidays, timeshare and "second homes" on the island. But your poster could be on any island theme – agriculture, fishing, the volcanic landscape, conservation, etc.

advertisements. As you can see, most of the advertisements are for land and property. But look also at those for English-speaking bars, shops and language classes. Why do you think there is a need for both English and Spanish classes on the island?

Urbanizaciónes

The Spanish call the new holiday villages *urbanizaciónes*. This really means "housing estates", but the homes found in them are very different from those in, for example, Arrecife's municipal housing estates, or in the island's old

agricultural and fishing villages. Figure 64 is a plan of the Las Casitas *urbanización* at Playa Blanca (Sur). Las Casitas means "the small houses", but these forty-five modern dwellings built by *Wimpey* are far larger than those occupied by the majority of islanders. They are all equipped with luxury bathrooms and electrical "mod cons", and each home has the use of the swimming pool and landscaped gardens.

64 A new tourist development at Playa Blanca (Sur). As well as a swimming pool and landscaped gardens around the villas, what other things are there in Las Casitas that you would not expect to find in the island's traditional villages? What are the features and buildings of the agricultural and fishing villages that are not found in Las Casitas?

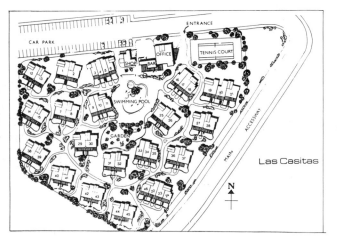

Las Casitas

65 At Jameo del Agua part of an old volcanic tube has been turned into a tourist attraction.

Many of the homes in the new holiday villages like Las Casitas are owned by a method called "Timeshare". This means they have many owners, people who buy ownership for just one or more weeks of the year for their lifetime. Of course, some of the villas and apartments are bought outright by single owners who either live in them permanently or let out their properties to holiday companies. But for those unable to afford the full purchase price, "Timeshare" is a relatively cheap way for foreigners to buy a share of a Lanzarote holiday property. This entitles them to use it at the same fixed times every year. Many "Timeshare" schemes are the combined developments of property firms and air companies. The latter provide charter flights to the island, as Lanzarote has no regular scheduled flights from countries such as Britain and Germany. Look at Figure 63 again. It says something about "Timeshare". What message is the cartoon trying to convey?

As you can imagine, "Timeshare" needs careful organization. Most holiday *urbanizaciónes* have an administrative office and a resident staff deals which with bookings, cleaning and repairs. Such jobs now provide many of the islanders with work. Others are employed in tending the gardens and other communal facilities such as the local shop and bar.

Caring for the island

The *conejos* are proud of their island. They have been planning its landscape for a very long time. They do not want to see Lanzarote ruined by over-commercialization, as has happened to some parts of Tenerife and Gran Canaria. Yet they realize the advantages that tourism is bringing to a poor island. The policy of the *Cabildo*, therefore, is strict planning control.

Protected Areas

Many parts of Lanzarote are now protected from development. These are the areas of outstanding natural scenery, or those where rare species of flora and fauna survive. As we has seen, the salt pans of Janubio are home to many species of local and migratory birds, and the Famara region, especially its coastal cliffs, has many species of rare plants. In fact, most of the native plants of the island can be found here.

The largest protected area is the National Park of Timanfaya where the "Fire Mountains" are located. The park was founded in 1974 and it covers 12,620 acres of lava fields, volcanic cones and craters. As in all national parks there are rules and instructions to follow, and visitors are taken around by guides, usually in special buses. These follow the 14 kilometre-long *Ruta de los Volcanes* (the Route of the Volcanoes) through the park. For the botanist there are many species of lichen which, together with succulents, have colonized these dry volcanic lands. But there is also a shrub called *aulaga*. For the benefit of visitors the guide sets its dead branches alight by dropping it into a specially dug hole in the hot ground surface. The main animals are reptiles. The most common is the Atlantic lizard which is found on all the Canaries.

New developments are encouraged, but only if they blend with and enhance the island's landscape.

Most of the holiday accommodation is in villas, bungalows and apartments and, as we have seen, they are arranged in carefully planned villages in garden settings. The island does have a number of new hotels, but there is now a law which limits the height of buildings. The only high-rise development (nine storeys) in the whole of the island is the Gran Hotel in Arrecife. This was one of the first new hotels to be built. It dominates Arrecife's seafront and is visible from many parts of the island's south coast. It is regarded by many as a monument to what commercial development might have been like throughout the island had not building restrictions been enforced. Outside of Arrecife no new building can be more than four storeys high. In the city itself, because of the shortage of land, buildings can be higher, but planning control is still strictly enforced.

As well as controlling the height of buildings, the *Cabildo* advises on architectural styles. All new buildings have to blend with the island's traditional architecture and unique landscape. If possible, local building materials are used in new constructions and even colour schemes

66 Much is being done to improve the appearance of Arrecife. Here workmen are laying new pavements in the centre of the city.

are carefully checked. What do you think of this idea of colour control? Why are white and green regarded as the most appropriate colours? In addition, visitors to Lanzarote will see few roadside advertisements, and flashing neon signs are not encouraged. No litter is allowed on the beaches, and even in Arrecife the streets are remarkably clean.

César Manrique

The man who has been largely responsible for overseeing the island's development is César Manrique (see page 35). Born on Lanzarote in 1920, he is an artist and sculptor of international fame. Today he is also "artistic consultant" to the *Cabildo* and his objective is to blend tourism and other new developments with the island's natural surroundings. He calls himself an "ecological artist" and, wherever possible, he uses natural stones and other objects in his designs. This he has done in his own home, which is a modern villa built partly below the ground in a series of volcanic caves.

Elsewhere on the island Manrique has been responsible for holiday villages, road-building, public housing, gardens and even the design of litter bins. But some of his most famous projects are those built as tourist attractions. At the Cueva de los Verdes (see page 23) and the nightclub of Jameo del Agua he has combined natural beauty with man's artistry. Also on the Famara cliffs Manrique has transformed an old look-out fort into a restaurant and observation centre, with magnificent views across to Graciosa and the other small islands. Much of the layout of the Timanfaya National Park is again his work, as is the design of the Contemporary Art Museum in the old fort of San José. But most visitors to the island are first introduced to the work of Manrique at the airport. His design for the passenger lounge is really splendid. It has the appearance and atmosphere of a large, cool tent filled with tropical ferns and other plants. All the decoration is in the island's colours – green and white.

Communications

The tourist industry has greatly improved communications to, and within, the island. The airport, 5 km to the south of Arrecife, has daily scheduled flights to Fuerteventura, Gran Canaria and Tenerife. From the latter two airports there are flight connections to La Palma and Hierro (Gomera has no airport), and to major mainland Spanish cities. Today Lanzarote's airport is extremely busy with daily (and nightly) charter flights. These bring visitors from many European countries and other parts of the world. In fact, if tourism continues to grow at its present rate, it will not be long before the island's visitors, at any one time, outnumber the local inhabitants.

Others still visit Lanzarote by ship, either on scheduled services from European ports, especially Cadiz, or on cruise liners that call at Los Mármoles, Arrecife's passenger and commercial port. All the Canaries are connected by inter-island boat services. Very popular with the *conejos* is the regular line that operates between Arrecife and Puerto de la Luz (Las Palmas). As the largest city in the Canaries, Las Palmas has an attractive range of entertainments and many large department stores with goods that are not available on Lanzarote.

As we saw in Chapter 1 Lanzarote is not a particularly mountainous island, so road-building is relatively easy. There are over 120 km of main roads and a complicated system of minor ones and rural tracks. The latter, however, are usually in a bad state of repair and suitable only for pedestrian and animal transport. The main road network branches out from Arrecife, whose busy bus station serves all the main island villages and also the tourist resorts. Bus timetables operate to serve the islanders rather than the tourists. Many islanders arrive in Arrecife early in the morning to work, visit the market or to conduct other business. Some return home late at night, for the more isolated communities have only one bus service to and from Arrecife each day.

Planning Arrecife

Compared to what it was less than twenty years ago, Arrecife is a prosperous and fast-growing city. It now has a population of around 30,000. This is more than half the island's total, not including the holiday-makers. The city is the centre of the island's business, and many people from the countryside are moving to the capital in search of jobs. Everywhere new building is in progress, especially council *urbanizaciónes*. But the *Cabildo* is anxious that Arrecife does not become a city of urban sprawl. Most of the estates are well-designed and form local communities with easy access to the city centre. Probably the biggest problem today is traffic, despite the one-way system and pedestrianized areas.

Arrecife's waterfront has been laid out as attractive promenades and gardens. These are the city's social centres during evenings and, especially, at weekends. Although it is not one of the island's main tourist resorts, there are plans to improve Arrecife's beaches and to build more hotels and other holiday accommodation. Already many new bars, clubs and restaurants have opened in the narrow streets behind the waterfront.

With its shops, offices, banks, supermarkets and restaurants, Arrecife is a good place to meet the people of Lanzarote. By far the best time to be in the city is during the festival of San Ginés, the island's patron saint. The islanders will tell you that not only does he protect them from natural disasters, but also is responsible for the many changes affecting Lanzarote today. They agree, of course, that there are many others interested in the island's welfare. These are the more local saints that are prayed to in the small village churches scattered throughout "Fire Island".

Island Festivals

Like all the Canaries, Lanzarote has many festivals (*fiestas*) and a number of important pilgrimages (*romerías*) to special churches. On 15 September pilgrimage is made to the small village of Mancha Blanca to the south of Tinajo. Here, the story goes, the Virgin commanded a lava flow to stop, thus saving the people from destruction. A church was built – Our Lady of the Volcanoes – where special services are held to thank the Virgin.

Other important festivals are those of the Virgin del Carmen in Teguise, San Antonia in Tias and San Ginés in Arrecife. As patron saint of the island, San Ginés' festival has been declared an event of special tourist interest. During 24-29 August the Arrecife waterfront, close to the saint's church, is crowded with people eating and drinking from temporary stalls. There are rides and other amusements for children, and also Canary music and dancing. Musical groups come from all parts of the island to take part in contests. One of the most successful of these folk groups is *Aley* from San Bartolomé. It has won many local and national competitions. An instrument used in all Canary Island music is the *timple*, which is a small guitar still made by local craftsmen in Teguise. During the festival of San Ginés the Queen of Festivities is elected and she parades through Arrecife in a camel caravan of beautifully decorated carts. An impressive firework display takes place on the last night of the celebrations.

11

Lanzarote-present and future

Having read the previous chapters you will now be able to summarize Lanzarote's main characteristics. To begin with, what would you say are the main features of the island's natural environment? How have the things you list influenced the life of the *conejos*, and in what ways have the *conejos* changed their environment to make their lives easier and better? You will probably agree that the natural environment still presents many difficult problems. In your opinion what are the greatest natural problems facing the islanders today?

The previous chapters have also shown how Lanzarote is changing. For many centuries it was an isolated, little-known and very poor island. However, there were periods in its history when some of the islanders grew rich. What were the main occupations and products that brought wealth to the island? Are there any ways in which they could bring money to the island again? For example, how could the lives of the Lanzarote fishermen be improved, and do you think the island's agriculture could be made more profitable?

The island's isolation is now at an end. This is one of the biggest changes the island is experiencing. What is the main cause of this, and do you think it is a good thing? As we have seen, life in some of the coastal villages is greatly different from what it was a few decades ago. But in other parts of the island life remains primitive and, despite the ingenious methods by the farmers to grow crops, agriculture is backward.

Lanzarote is still a poor island. Like the rest of the Canaries, its unemployment level is far higher than the average for Spain. Recently, too, the cost of living has been rising by 30 per cent per annum. What do you think is one of the causes of this inflation? Why, if more jobs are being provided by tourism, are there so many islanders out of work? One of the reasons is to do with Lanzarote's rapidly growing population.

Improved medical facilities and a better diet mean that the island's birth rate is increasing and its death rate falling. Jobs are already scarce in farming and fishing and, as we have seen, many people are leaving their villages to work in the new tourist resorts. But many of these jobs in tourism are filled by more experienced people who move to Lanzarote and the other islands from the Spanish mainland. These *peninsulares*, much to the annoyance of the islanders, get large pay supplements from the Spanish government for working in the islands. In spite of the importance of tourism, therefore, there are many young people who have to move from Lanzarote to Spain, or abroad, to get jobs.

The fact remains that tourism is now Lanzarote's main growth area – the new "life-blood" of the island. But is it the real answer to the island's problems? Already it is the cause of rapid price rises. What do you think would happen to Lanzarote if the entire island were dependent on tourism? At present the island government is aware of the need for landscape conservation and tourism management. It realizes that Lanzarote's individuality is the island's main attraction. Uncontrolled tourism destroys the very thing most tourists are looking for – a place that is different and full of personality. Lanzarote is both these things and its future very much depends on the way the island is being planned today.

67 The waterfront at Arrecife is now a landscaped promenade. It is a popular strolling-ground in the evenings.

Glossary

acid lava   Thick lava with a large amount of the silica mineral. It flows slowly and cools quickly

active volcanoes   Volcanoes in the process of erupting

alluvial fans   Material deposited by a stream where it flows from a steep valley into an open plain

aquifer   A formation of rocks that holds water underground

archipelago   A group of islands

autonomous region   A region having its own government

banks   Sections of the continental shelf where ocean water is shallower

basalt   A common rock poured out as molten magma

basic lava   A more liquid lava with smaller amounts of the silica mineral. It flows quickly and cools slowly

composite volcanoes   Those made of various layers of lava and pyroclasts

condensation   The change from a gaseous to a liquid state

continental islands   Islands found on, and part of, continental shelves

continental shelves   Shallow areas on the sea-bottom, bordering the continents

co-ordinates   Lines of latitude and longitude used to locate a point on the earth's surface

crater   The funnel-shaped hollow at the summit, or on the side, of a volcano

crust (earth's)   The outer layer of the solid earth

cultivation terraces   Man-made terraces on hillsides for growing crops

desert   A region with a shortage of water and a thin vegetation cover

desalination   The process of removing salt

diurnal winds   Daily winds caused by differences in pressure over the land and sea

dormant volcanoes   Those not erupting but which could erupt at any time

drought   A long period with a shortage of rainfall

dry farming   Use of land specially prepared and farmed to overcome a water shortage

ecology   The study of the links between organisms and their environment

ecosystem   The interaction of organisms and environment

environment   Natural surrounding; a region; a landscape

erosion   The way in which the earth's surface is worn away by natural agencies, e.g. water, wind, ice.

evaporation   The change from a liquid state to a vapour

faults and fractures   Large breaks in the earth's crust

fissure   A long narrow crack in a rock

fumarole   An opening in the ground through which steam and other gases escape

geothermal   Heat in the interior of the earth

Great Age of Discovery   The discovery and colonization of the New World during the 15th and 16th centuries

humus   Organic material in a soil on which a soil's fertility depends

infiltration   The passage of a fluid (e.g. water) into the pores of a solid (e.g. rock)

irrigation   Supplying farmland with water by means of artificial channels and streams

land bridge   The former land link between an island and a nearby continent

landscape   Scenery; environment

lava   Molten rock or magma that escapes from a volcanic cone or fissure

lichen   A plant that is a cross between a fungus and an algae

magma   Molten material found under the earth's crust

mantle (earth's)   The layer of material lying between the earth's crust and the earth's core

meridian   A line of longitude
Mid-Atlantic Ridge   A great belt of submarine ranges and chasms
mollusc   A soft-bodied animal, usually with a hard shell (e.g. mussel or oyster)
municipality   A city, town or district with its own local self-government
ocean deep   The deepest part of an ocean
oceanic island   An island, usually volcanic, that rose independently from the floor of an ocean
ornithology   The study of birds and their behaviour
orographical rain   Rain caused by mountains forcing moist air to rise
palaeomagnetic survey   The study and measurement of magnetism in rocks
permeable   Allowing water to soak through soil and rock (opposite, impermeable)
plankton   Small plant and animal particles floating in sea water, usually invisible to the naked eye
plates   Huge moving sections that make up the earth's crust
porous   Able to absorb air and water etc (opposite, non-porous)
promontory   A high point of land that juts into the sea
pyroclasts   Small pieces of solidified lava ejected by volcanoes
radioactivity   Radiation from atomic nuclei
radiometric survey   The study and measurement of radiant energy
rain shadow   An area of less rainfall on the side of a mountain away from the main wind direction
relative humidity   The ratio of the amount of water vapour in the air compared to the largest amount
     possible at a given temperature
rennet   A substance used for curdling milk in cheesemaking
saline   Containing salt
saturation level   The level to which a soil or a rock (for example) is filled with water
sea-floor spreading   The way in which oceans increase in size as new material escapes from submarine
     ridges and chasms
sedimentary rocks   Rocks formed by the wearing away of older rocks. The eroded material is laid down
     as sediments which harden into rocks
soil   The top layer of the earth's land surface composed of rock particles, humus, air and water
structural axis   The structure of the geology underground that controls surface landforms
subduction zone   Parts of the earth's crust where the edges of plates are returned to the earth's mantle
succulent plant   A plant in dry areas that stores water in its fleshy leaves or stems
topography   The surface landforms of a region
transpiration   The process of plants losing moisture through the stomata (pores) of their leaves
Tropic of Cancer   The line of latitude at 23.5° north of the equator
Utopia   A place considered to be perfect or ideal
volcanic cone   The conical hill or mountain formed by a volcanic eruption
volcanic tube   Formed when a flow of lava solidifies on contact with the air and ground. The outer surface
     crusts over, but the lava inside drains out to leave a hollow tube
water table   The level below which the ground of any area is saturated with water
weathering   The way in which rocks etc are broken down by the elements of weather, especially changes
     in temperature
xerophyte   Plants able to survive in dry areas

SPANISH WORDS USED IN THE TEXT

Spanish	English	Spanish	English	Spanish	English
agua	water	enarenado	special Lanzarote field	picón	volcanic lapilli
alijibe	water cistern	gavia	small dam	playa	beach
bahía	bay	geria	cultivated hollow	puente	bridge
arrecife	reef	golfo	gulf	puerto	port
barranco	gully, ravine	infierno	hell	punta	headland, promontory
cabildo	town council	isla	isle/island	roque	rock
charco	pool (harbour)	islote	islet	queso	cheese
conejera	rabbit warren	jable	sand-covered area	refugio	refuge/shelter
conejo	rabbit	jameos	surface holes (volcanic)	salina	salt pan
conquistador	conqueror			San	saint
costa	coast	lagunetas	small ponds	urbanización	housing estate
cueva	cave	llano	plain (lowland)	volcán	volcano
desierta	desert	malpaís	"badland"		
		montaña	mountain		

Further reading

Guidebooks:

Most of the books written in English on the Canary Islands are general guidebooks for visitors. Some of these provide a great deal of background information on the history, geography and landscapes of the islands. The following are useful:

A. Pink and P. Watkins, *See Madeira and the Canaries* (Format, 1967)
H. Myhill, *The Canary Islands* (Faber, 1972)
A. and M. Tisdall, *Gran Canaria and the Eastern Canary Islands* (Roger Lascelles, 1984)
N. Rochford, *Landscapes of Tenerife* (Sunflower Books, 1984)
N. Rochford, *Landscapes of Gran Canaria* (Sunflower Books, 1986)

Academic books:

D. and Z. Bramwell, *Wild Flowers of the Canary Islands* (Stanley Thornes, 1974)
J. Mercer, *The Canary Islands* (Rex Collings, 1980)
J. Mercer, *Fuerteventura* (David and Charles, 1973)
S.L. Herrera, *The Canary Islands through History* (Madrid, 1978)

Books in Spanish:

There are many books on the Canary Islands written in Spanish. Most can be bought only in Spain. The two mentioned below provide a great deal of information on the islands. They also provide a good way of learning/practising Spanish.

P.H. Hernández, *Natura y Cultura de Las Islas Canarias* (Las Palmas, 1978)
   (This is a well-illustrated book dealing with all aspects of the physical and human geography of the islands)
Editorial Interinsular Canaris S.A., *Atlas Basico de Canaris* (Santa Cruz, 1980)
   (This is a beautifully-produced thematic atlas of the islands)

Maps:

Detailed maps of Lanzarote and the other Canaries are available in many British bookshops.

Island Information

Area: 795 sq km (the main island)
836 sq km (Lanzarote and its islands to the north)

Capital: Arrecife, situated in the centre of the island's southern coast.

Official language: Spanish (*Español*). There is a distinct Canary Island accent and many Spanish words and expressions from the New World.

Currency: *Pesetas* (*Ptas*). The *peseta* is divided into 100 *céntimos* (*cénts*). *Cénts* are rarely used as their value is too small to worry about.

Government: The *Cabildo Insular* is the local government of Lanzarote. The island forms part of the province of *Las Palmas de Gran Canaria*. The two Canary Island provinces form the Spanish autonomous region of *Las Islas Canaries*. This means that they are self-governing, but still part of the Kingdom of Spain (*Reino de España*).

Official flag: This is the flag of the Kingdom of Spain. The outside bands are red, and the broader inside band is yellow. Sometimes the royal coat of arms appears on the yellow band. Lanzarote also has its own coat of arms. This is a shield with ancient Guanche vessels on it. On the top is a royal crown.

Population: 51,271 (estimated 1987). Sixty per cent now live in and around Arrecife. The inland villages are losing their population. The coastal resorts are rapidly expanding.

Religion: The national religion of Spain (and the Canary Islands) is Roman Catholicism. Catholic and Protestant services are also held in foreign languages.

Economy: Lanzarote's traditional farming and fishing economy is changing rapidly. The most important economic sector is now tourism. This is also leading to important social changes and many new planning developments. The main exports are agricultural and fish products. Fuel supplies are the main imports.

Important dates:

1336 Lancelotto Malocello's expedition to Lanzarote
1341 Niccolosa da Rocca's expedition to Lanzarote
1402 Jean de Béthencourt's arrival on Lanzarote
1404 Lanzarote is made the seat of a Catholic bishopric
1470 Portugal cedes the Canary Islands to Castille and Aragon
1492 Christopher Columbus uses the Canaries as a base for his New World explorations
1496 The conquest of Tenerife which gave all the Canaries to Spain
16-18th centuries Forts built to protect Lanzarote from invaders
1730-36 Great volcanic eruptions on Lanzarote
1823 The Canaries become a single province of Spain
1842 Lanzarote's last volcanic eruption
1852 The Canaries are made "open" or "duty free" ports
1883 A submarine telegraph cable connects the Canaries with Spain
1898 Spain loses many of its New World colonies
1927 Two separate Canary provinces are created
1975 Formation of the present Kingdom of Spain

Index

The Conservative Party

AN ILLUSTRATED HISTORY